Defender of Faith

A Special Note

"**Thank you** for reading *Defender of Faith*. I hope you're encouraged and inspired by this book to live out your journey with God front and center, and enjoy all he has to offer. My prayer is that you will be courageous along the way and become the person God created you to be as you trust in his perfect plan for your life. Enjoy the ride!"

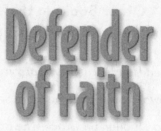

Mike Fisher

**Other Books in the
Zonderkidz Biography Series:**

Gifted Hands: The Ben Carson Story

Toward the Goal: The Kaká Story

Breaking Through by Grace: The Bono Story

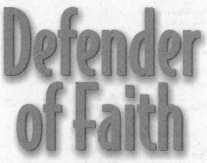

Defender of Faith

the
Mike Fisher
Story

Kim Washburn

ZONDERVAN.com/
AUTHORTRACKER
follow your favorite authors

For my Jakeb and my parents

ZONDERKIDZ

Defender of Faith: The Mike Fisher Story
Copyright © 2011 by Kim Washburn

This title is also available as a Zondervan ebook.
Visit www.zondervan.com/ebooks

Requests for information should be addressed to:

Zonderkidz, *Grand Rapids, Michigan* 49530

Library of Congress Cataloging-in-Publication Data

Washburn, Kim, 1970–
    Defender of faith : the Mike Fisher story / Kim Washburn.
        p. cm. – (ZonderKidz biography)
        ISBN 978-0-310-72540-4 (pbk.)
    1. Fisher, Mike, 1980– –Juvenile literature. 2. Hockey players–Canada–Biography–
Juvenile literature. 3. Christian athletes–United States–x Biography–Juvenile literature.
4. Christian athletes–Religious life. I. Title.
    GV848.5.F5W37 2011
    796.962092–dc23
    [B]   2011018126

Art direction: Ben Fetterley
Cover design: Kris Nelson and Mark Veldheer
Cover photo: John Russell/NHLI via Getty Images
Back cover photos: Photo in Nashville jersey: Frederick Breedon/Getty Images; Photo as child and with girls: Photo provided by Jim and Karen Fisher; Mike Fisher and Carrie Underwood: Larry Busacca/Getty images for NARAS
Interior design and composition: Greg Johnson/Textbook Perfect

Printed in the United States of America

11 12 13 14 15 16 17 18 /DCI/ 23 22 21 20 19 18 17 16 15 14 13 12 11 10 9 8 7 6 5

Table of Contents

Some Kind of Pain

March 16, 2006

Hockey is many things. Wimpy is not one of them.

In early 2006, the Ottawa Senators were in a race for the playoffs. They were the highest-scoring team in the National Hockey League (NHL), scoring nearly four goals per game. By the middle of March, the Senators had won eight of their last nine games. And veteran Mike Fisher had scored and scrapped all season to help his team become one of the favorites to challenge for the Stanley Cup.

On March 16, the Senators were in Boston, down a goal and down a man on the penalty kill. Fisher intercepted the puck and carried it the length of the ice, driving to the net.

A Bruin defenseman picked him up on the wing, cutting off his angle to the net. Together they skidded by the goal line. Mike's right leg got caught for a split second and bent as he fell to the ice. With his leg folded behind him, he slid into the end boards. When he hit the wall, his body tensed as his twisted ankle took the brunt of the force.

Grimacing, Mike got to his knees, stood up slowly, and tried to skate. But his ankle couldn't take the weight. He knelt on the ice, his face stressed in pain.

The announcer calling the game knew it was bad news. "One thing you know about Mike Fisher is he's not going to lay around the ice," he said, watching the trainer come out to help with the injury. "He'd get himself off. He had to be in some kind of pain ... That is one guy you can *not* afford to lose at this time of the season."

Ottawa Sun hockey writer Bruce Garrioch wrote, "I nearly cried when I saw Fisher go down."

He wasn't the only one.

SensNation — red-wearing, towel-waving fans of the team — loved the gritty, hardworking passion of number twelve. His teammates needed his aggressive speed on both ends of the ice. And for Mike, the only thing more painful than playing the postseason on a broken ankle would be missing it altogether.

Mike had to be helped off the ice and back into the training room. It would be easy to cave to all the bad news — the sharp pain of the ankle, a long injury that could keep him from challenging for the Cup, the ache of watching the ultimate competition from the sidelines.

Mike Fisher (#12) skates along the boards past Brad Stuart (#6) of the Boston Bruins.

Mike glanced at the game clock on the wall and tried to hold on to something encouraging.

Ticking down the seconds of the game, the digital clock on the wall paused for a stoppage of play with twelve minutes, twelve seconds left in the game.

12:12. Mike did a double take. "Right away I thought Romans 12:12: 'Be glad for all God is planning for you. Be patient in trouble, and always be prayerful.'"[1]

With a deep breath, Mike refocused—but not on his circumstances of an injury. Instead, he focused on the promise of his faith. After all, he was more than a hockey player. He was first a follower of God. Here in a lonely training room on the road, Mike's faithful God reminded him of a tender truth. "It was kind of just God saying, 'You know what? Be patient and trust in me and lean on me and things will work out.'"[2]

And they did. To the amazement of everyone who winced at the replay and squinted at the slow motion footage, Mike's ankle wasn't broken. "I got back in less than three weeks, which was surprising to me," he admitted.[3]

After more than ten years in professional sports, Mike knows as well as anyone that pressures and distractions can come as fast as a slap shot. So how does somebody maintain focus on what's truly important in the middle of tough circumstances—slumps, criticism, contracts, expectations, injuries, ego, media ...?

Mike's unwavering focus stems from his faith in God. Planted first by his family, his faith grew into the stabilizing force in his life. But it didn't happen overnight. Cultivating strength of character and conviction when surroundings are unpredictable takes serious training and practice. And Mike has had plenty.

After all, hockey is many things. But wimpy isn't one of them.

2

Where It All Started

1980s

On June 5, 1980, the New York Islanders had a Stanley Cup, nineteen-year-old Wayne Gretzky had played only one NHL season, and Ottawa hadn't had a pro hockey team for forty-six years. None of that concerned Jim and Karen Fisher, who were welcoming their newborn son, Michael Andrew. By 1987, the Fishers had a full house in Peterborough, Ontario, with their children Rob, Mike, Meredith, and Bud.

For the Fisher family, faith was significant and central. They worshiped at church. They prayed at home. They said grace before meals and at bedtime. Watching his parents live out their faith, Mike was captivated by Christ early. "When I was six years old, I made the step of faith to accept him into my heart," he said. "I remember

The Fisher Family, 1991 (l to r): Mike, Meredith, Rob, Bud, Karen, and Jim

I prayed with my mom before I went to school. I didn't want to wait any longer."[1]

Feeling honored and lucky to have a relationship with Jesus, Mike humbly realized the gift of salvation. His faith was young, but his belief was grounded in a heart where it would grow. "It's hard to do it on your own," he acknowledged later. "A lot of people and Christian friends and family and people around me are praying for me, encouraging me, and walking along with me."[2]

Mike's faith started early. So did his love of hockey. Watching Gretzky dominate was cool. Wearing a Montreal jersey was neat. Cheering for the closest Canadian team, the Toronto Maple Leafs, was good. But really, Mike wanted to *play*.

Big brother Rob could compete, and Mike wanted to keep up with him. When Bud came along seven years after Mike, the Fisher boys had their goalie. "We'd just put pads on him, because we wanted someone to shoot on downstairs in the basement."

Mike's dad worked in the family-owned business, and his mom was a nurse, but they soon realized that supporting their kids and shuttling them to their activities was a full-time job. So Mom retired to stay home. "They were there to support me and take me where I needed to go," Mike realized, "and it was a total act of selflessness."

With four active kids at all ages, they hustled from one thing to the next. At one point, the Fishers had three boys in hockey and a daughter in either synchronized swimming or figure skating. "It was just go, go, go," said Mike. "But dinner was still important, and we'd try to sit down as a family. Sometimes after we'd do a little bit of a devotional, get into the Bible. That was an important thing for us."

When it came to competing, the Fishers really just wanted their kids to have fun. "My parents were pretty relaxed, let me make my decisions where I wanted to play and when I wanted to play."[3] Eventually the Fisher kids chose different things. Rob got interested in things other than hockey in high school. Bud was a goaltender at Quinnipiac University, where he received a good education. Mike played some baseball and volleyball— loved to compete in anything, really—but he excelled in hockey. And he played it all the time.

One summer, the Fishers took a rare break from the rink for a road trip. They packed up their ten-passenger Chevy van, hooked up a pop-up camper, and headed west to Vancouver. They traveled 4,500 miles across Canada. On the way back home, they took the southern scenic route through the United States. It was a uniquely long vacation for the Fishers and a long haul for the Chevy. "We had a couple spots where the van broke down," Mike remembered. "So we'd pull off. My dad would fix it, and we'd be on [our way] again."[4]

The Fisher family hit the odd hotel, but mostly they stayed in camping spots along the way. Watching the changing countryside, Mike looked for wildlife he'd never seen in person—elk, moose, black bear. The boys competed to spot the animals. "I don't remember who won any of the competitions," he grinned. "Probably me."

Photo provided by Jim and Karen Fisher

Mike, age 7

And his sister? "She would just read Nancy Drew books in the back,"[5] Mike laughed.

They watched out the windows and played cards. Rob drove and Meredith read (and read and read). And while the outdoors was a highlight for Mike, so was each NHL rink they found along the way. If they passed through a city with one, they found it, piled out, and took a Fisher family photo.

That road trip was a special, long vacation. But the Fishers also had plenty of recreation at home in the wide-open cottage country of Ontario.

Mike's mom grew up one of nine children in the Bancroft area. It was there she first met Mike's dad at Graphite Bible Camp. With extended family still there, Mike spent time in that area snowmobiling, four-wheeling, playing pond hockey, and hunting with his uncles and cousins. "Every fall, I used to try and get away for a day or two and go, as a kid," Mike remembered. "That was my favorite time of the year, no question."[6]

The chilly first two weeks in November were hunting season. "It wasn't just the hunting part," he explained. "It was the camaraderie of the guys and hanging out in hunt camp. Those types of things were really cool."[7]

For the Fishers, hunting brought the family and guys together to connect, reflect, and enjoy the wild creation of God. For Mike specifically, his love of the outdoors started with exploring on his own, fishing as a family, or joining his dad and uncles for hunting. And it only grew from there.

Because they visited Graphite Road during the year, hunted the area, and shared some of the Christmas break together, the Fishers stayed close with extended family. When Mike was in his teens, his older cousin Warren started going to college in Peterborough. Instead of commuting an hour and a half to Bancroft, Warren lived with the Fishers and shared a room with Mike. A strong Christian and good role model, Warren became like another big brother.

After dinner, Warren and the boys would head downstairs. In the basement was a full-sized net and a pretty good hockey area, so they'd shoot pucks, tennis balls, whatever. "One of us would be goalie," Mike remembered, "or we'd throw Bud in net."[8]

When Mike began junior hockey, Warren was still living with the family. Mike's move four hours away meant Warren had a room to himself. But they would live together again. And Mike would take away a lot more than a good, post-dinner hockey contest.

Surrounded by family and friends, Mike was encouraged to enjoy his relationship with God and run with it. "My parents always stressed faith as a central part of my life, and I grew to understand the importance of having a balance in life and finding a purpose through our Creator. I believe we are all gifted in certain areas and it's our responsibility to use these gifts that God has given us for his glory."[9]

Mike didn't know what his future held, but he was excited about who held it. "It's great having God to rely on, knowing he has a plan for us. We don't have to worry what's going to go on in our future or what's going to happen down the road."[10] His family helped plant faith and focus. Blessed with determination and drive, Mike would use these gifts to the fullest.

3

Make It or Break It

Junior League, 1997–1999

There are few places on earth where a single sport is woven into the fabric of a culture. For Canadians, hockey is that sport. Lifelong fans know the ins and outs of box scores, the science of plus/minus ratings, and the discipline behind the fight card. Peewee programs, junior levels, drafts, select teams, divisional leagues—Canadian hockey is serious fun and intense entertainment.

Maybe it's true that the kids in Peterborough are born with hockey sticks in their hands. Many NHL players have grown up around the area. Mike watched Tie Domi, Chris Pronger, Mike Ricci, and Cory Stillman when they played for the Petes of the Ontario Hockey League. Legendary coach Roger Neilson was a Peterborough celebrity. He led the Peterborough Petes to seven consecutive winning seasons and gained a reputation as a hockey whiz and innovator. His knowledge of the game actually led to rule changes. Thanks to Neilson, goalies can no longer leave sticks across the crease before being pulled out for another player. Thanks to Neilson, a rushing defenseman can't be used in place of a goalie on a penalty shot.[1]

Mike grew up in this competitive culture—and loved it. In the all-Ontario Finals, teams traveled to Sudbury to play for the Household Cup. So at the age of thirteen, he traveled four hours with his team to play for the same prize won by many of hockey's champions. It was a big deal at the time, and Mike thought he could get used to the thrill of regular, intense competition.

If someone needed to find Mike (nicknamed Fish), it wasn't a question of *what* he was doing, only *where*—basement hockey, road hockey, pond hockey, summer Central Ontario Select teams, hockey camps, organized games, spur-of-the-moment competitions.

In a culture where hockey is equal to religion for many people, sometimes kids outside the Fisher family didn't understand where church and God fit in. What good reason—other than a body cast—could there be to miss a practice or important game? "It wasn't (so) much bullying as teasing," Mike explained. "Some kids don't understand why you'd go to church. Some kids would poke fun at you."[2]

While other kids might have crumbled at the adversity, the teasing had the opposite effect on Mike. It made him *more determined*. "That kind of motivated me, I think, when people didn't understand or poked fun."[3] Instead of letting it discourage or distract him, it fueled him.

Ultimately he brought his tough play on the ice, and the talking and teasing quieted down. "As a kid, obviously, being a Christian was tough," Mike remembered. "I went through some struggles, challenges where certain individuals, when I was younger, didn't understand why I was a Christian and why I believed in the Bible, and sometimes maybe I missed a practice or something to attend church. I was made fun of as a kid, and that really challenged me and made me stronger as a person to want to play hockey the best I can and still be a Christian and not be a soft player, but play hard and be competitive."[4]

Easygoing off the ice, nothing was soft about his hockey. An offensive force once his skates were laced, Mike drove himself harder than an old Zamboni. His wrister, speed, grit, and work ethic helped him shine in a league of standouts. "A lot of it is my God-given abilities," Fisher said. "We're all given different things, and I think one of them is the determination I have. I don't take my health for granted, and try to give it everything I have when I can."[5]

When Mike was seventeen, he was a second round pick in the 1997 Priority Selection. For the season, he went to play hockey in Sudbury, four hours from the comfort, familiarity, support, and good cooking of home.

Photo provided by Jim and Karen Fisher

Mike, age 17

Right before junior hockey, Mike's dad told his son to make the most of the time away. "These are the make-it-or-break-it years. They're going to shape where you want to be in hockey," he said. Mike didn't forget it, and he set out to use the competitive edge God blessed him with to make the most of it. "I just wanted to do the best that I could do. My parents were always there to support me."[6]

During his time in Sudbury, Mike lived with another good family with two boys of their own. His parents came to games here and there. But away from home, Mike had to grow up a bit. Balancing hockey and school was like lacing up skates with gloves on—no easy feat. There was plenty to learn as he managed the pressures of playing competitive hockey and the pressures of being a teenager. "I realized that Christianity would play a big part in my life at a young age, but I didn't really grasp the concept of a true relationship with God [yet]."[7]

He spent the hockey season in Sudbury, going to school with his teammates, and then going to practice and games after classes. When the hockey season ended around April, he packed his bags and went back to Peterborough for the rest of the semester.

Mike played with the Sudbury Wolves for two straight seasons. Just like his dad had predicted, the two years of junior hockey proved a great on-ice education.

One of his coaches, Tom Watt, had experience with Team Canada, two World Hockey Championships, and three Canada Cups. Under his lead, Mike gained important skills and depth to his game. "He taught me a lot about playing defensively and made my transition to the NHL much easier," Mike noted later.[8] In fact, under Watt's tutelage, Fish became an aggressive two-way forward—that is, he became an asset on both offense and defense.

In Mike's first year with the Wolves, he registered 49 points (24 goals, 25 assists). His second year, he more than doubled his numbers with 106 points (41 goals, 65 assists). With Coach Watt and the sweat and strength of the players, the Sudbury Wolves made it to the playoffs for the first time in three years.

Mike's fast feet, strong shot, and tough play got him onto the draft boards of many NHL teams. On the verge of realizing his dream, Mike still remembered the best advice he got as a young hockey player: "Have fun and don't try to put too much pressure on yourself."[9] With a +38 rating in the Ontario Hockey League, Mike did just that.

4

Big Time with the Big Boys

1999–2000

Mike entered the NHL entry draft between his two years
with the Sudbury Wolves. On June 27, 1998, Mike and
his family were in Buffalo, New York, to face this new
level together. "I remember being really nervous, and
kind of didn't really know what to expect. Going in as an
eighteen-year-old you're not sure where you're going to be
drafted," he said.[1] He could go anywhere—Canada, the
United States, an expansion team, an original-six franchise, a small market with small budget, or a big market
with big demands.

The Fishers settled in as the notoriously long first
round of the draft got underway. (In fact, the NHL
would later change the format of the draft so the first
round would be on the first day, and rounds two through
seven would be on day two.)

The teams evaluated Mike's game as a prospect for the NHL with a player profile including:

ASSETS: *Great on the forecheck and can kill penalties with aplomb. Owns good speed and is extremely tenacious. Has excellent two-way ability. Also possesses a great shot.*

FLAWS: *While capable of scoring, he's not a go-to guy on offense because he lacks consistency in that department. His rambunctious style can lead to injuries.*

CAREER POTENTIAL: *Quality two-way center.*[2]

Mike went to the Ottawa Senators in the second round, forty-fourth overall.

A big presence in the smallest NHL city, the Senators have an unusual, interrupted history. One of the first hockey clubs, they were established in 1883, won eleven Stanley Cups, and competed in the National Hockey League starting in 1917. But in 1934, the team disbanded amid financial problems. In 1992, the Senators returned to Canada's capital city as an expansion team. Seven years later, Mike Fisher became Ottawa's number twelve.

The year Mike was drafted, the Senators were first in the Northeast Division and second in the Eastern Conference. But history showed they had their work cut out for them—the Northeast Division, formerly known as the Adams Division, hadn't captured the Cup since 1993.

Mike was excited about his future. "In Ottawa, you get a bit of everything. Fans are great. I'm still close to home—a lot of friends here and family." He appreciated the personal advantages too. "After practice I can hunt and fish and do all those things. Not too many cities you can do that, so I'm pretty blessed, for sure."[3]

In his new home two-and-a-half hours from Peterborough, Mike would grow from prospect to star, private citizen to public celebrity. Through it all, his parents' words of wisdom would steer him: Put God at the center of life and everything else—relationships and career—will fall into place.[4]

Professional sports can often be as stable as balancing atop Jell-O. For Mike, God provides the balance and stability needed to not just survive in the unpredictable, ever-changing world of the NHL, but to thrive.

When Mike began his professional career with Ottawa in 1999, Ottawa's Jacques Martin had been the head coach for four years, and Daniel Alfredsson was the new team captain.

Mike put his head down and got to work. He developed individual skills at both ends of the ice, making good reads, and moving the puck quickly. "He's brought an element of speed and quickness to our team," remarked Coach Martin. "He's very good on the puck and he does a very good job forechecking."[5]

On the ice and off Mike proved himself a good teammate. White index cards taped on a locker room mirror showed Fish was in the top three of a team ping-pong tournament. He held his own in friendly team competition where a missed penalty shot meant losing a shirt. And he could take a joke as well as dish it out. "I always seem to get the 'N Sync [boy band] stickers on my helmet just in time for practice," he smiled.[6]

"The biggest thing in coming to Ottawa was to establish right up front what my lifestyle was going to be," he said. "They know I'm a Christian, and they respect that as long as you respect them."[7]

Mike's 1999–2000 season was filled with first experiences. On October 2, 1999, the puck dropped on Mike's first game. Twelve days later, he scored his first goal. Going coast-to-coast alongside a high-scoring teammate, Mike put it away in the top corner. "I looked at Shawn McEachern," he grinned. "He's still mad I didn't pass the puck."[8]

When he played his tenth pro game, he passed his first NHL test. (Ten games in the league count as a full season, a significant benchmark for a junior-aged player.) "I still have to play the way I've been playing, or even better, than in the first nine games," he said. "I'm happy to be here."[9]

Against Montreal on November 6, Mike scored his first game-winner. Two weeks later he had his first NHL fight against Atlanta.

"The one thing about Mike Fisher is that you know what he brings to the table every night," said head coach Jacques Martin. "He's intense, and night in and night out he's our most physical player when it comes to finishing checks."[10]

Big Time with the Big Boys

Frank Gunn/The Canadian Press/AP Images

Mike knows how to put on a good solid hit. Here he checks Toronto Maple Leafs center Matt Stajan during second-period NHL hockey action in Toronto on Saturday, Nov. 17, 2007.

After thirty-two games and nine points, Mike registered another first. On December 30 in a match against Boston, Mike took a hit on the inside of his knee and tore his anterior cruciate ligament (ACL). It was his first year-ending injury.

After the long climb to the pros, Mike suddenly found himself in the valley. "You always hope to establish yourself in your first year, but unfortunately, it didn't work out that way for me," he said.[11] Then he revealed how hardship affected him, much like it did when kids would tease him for being a Christian — it made him determined. "You worry about how it will affect your performance, but it also pushes you to work that much harder," he admitted.[12]

Mike drew on his faith for encouragement in disappointment, balance in uncertainty, and perspective in bad news. "I didn't expect to make it that young and everything was looking great," he said. "But then [the injuries] happened and it makes you understand that Jesus is really in charge. It's like he says, 'You don't take the reins, I do.' He's really in charge of my career and my life."[13]

After reconstructive surgery to repair his ACL, Mike was forced to watch the rest of the season and playoffs from the sidelines. In the first Battle of Ontario, the Senators lost to the Maple Leafs four games to two.

Mike's season didn't go the way he expected, but the rookie took away a powerful lesson about what's important, what can be controlled, and what can't. He could prepare diligently and work hard, but ultimately God held real power. So Mike worked on what he could and leaned on God for the rest.

Through his good and difficult first season, Mike grew stronger physically and spiritually. The extra muscle would serve him well, but his relationship with Christ would serve him always. It was a powerful lesson that he was blessed to learn early.

Welcome to the big leagues.

5

More Than Me, Me, Me

2000–2001

Here was the conundrum: play aggressively or stay healthy for eighty-two regular season games. Was it possible to skate the thin line between *both*? Mike's physical, gritty style along with his speed and intensity on the ice meant that injuries could simply be part of his career.

"I need to bring a physical edge to the game in order for me to be effective," he noted. "I've always enjoyed that part of hockey." At the same time, he acknowledged the other side of the line. "Avoiding an injury [is] certainly at the top of my list,"[1] he noted with a grin.

Mike worked hard to rehabilitate the knee and be physically and mentally ready for his second year in Ottawa. Like every summer, he prepared on his own. "I usually take two to four weeks off. A month tops."[2]

In his independent workouts he worked on speed. "I try to do a lot of plyometrics, like jumping and bounding. [Doing] sprints on a field, running hills helps.... Core stuff you can do every day."[3]

By opening day of training camp in September, Mike was ready for the physical tests—leg squats, hurdle agility hops, medicine ball exercises, and sprints.

On the ice, he held his own. By the end of October, Mike was regularly establishing himself on both ends of the ice, like his unassisted goal in a win against Pittsburgh and his tough stance in a win against Philadelphia. (When the Flyer's Daymond Langkow gave him a shot in the neutral zone, Mike answered the cheap shot by dropping his gloves. Langkow ended up going down with Mike on top.)

Fighting in hockey is nothing like fighting in other sports. Throwing a punch at an opponent in football, soccer, or basketball doesn't show toughness, grit, or competitive spirit—it shows bad sportsmanship and a weak attitude. But in hockey, fighting is part of the fabric of the game. It's penalized with minutes in the box so it's not a free-for-all, but it abides by certain unwritten rules. "Christians work hard," Mike explained. "You can still play tough as long as you're smart and not dirty about it."[4]

By the end of the season, Mike had doubled the number of games he played as well as doubled his number of points. Although sidelined for twenty-two games with a sprained ligament, he had seven goals, three game-winners, and twelve assists. And he recorded more than

Ottawa Senators' Mike Fisher and Carolina Hurricanes' Scott Walker fight during the second period of an NHL hockey game in Raleigh, N.C., Wednesday, Dec. 12, 2007.

two hits per game for a massive 129 total. Ottawa won the Northeast Division and was off to the playoffs.

In a rematch of the previous year's Battle of Ontario, Ottawa faced off against provincial rival Toronto. During the season, the Senators dominated the Maple Leafs, winning each of their four matchups. But the Sens, who scored at least four goals against the Leafs during the season, couldn't score at all in the first two games of the playoffs. The Leafs' goalie was in a zone, apparently seeing the puck as more of a beach ball.

Down two games, the Sens fought in game number three but lost in overtime (OT) 3−2. They had to win game four just to stay alive. Ottawa scored first and then watched their season slip away with Toronto's three goals.

"Growing up, I wasn't a huge Leafs fan," Mike admitted to local reporters. "I'd watch them because we always had them on the local station." Then he grinned tightly. "But now I can't stand 'em."[5]

As a public figure and property of a team, a professional athlete has more than his position to consider. He has a "game" to play off the ice as well. Outside opinion and media scrutiny become part of the gig.

Just like every other new athlete, Mike had to learn as he went along. How could he be part of the community without getting lost in the demands and distractions? How could he balance expectations of teammates, coaches, owners, and fans? Yes, he was a Christian, but what did that look like in the NHL?

So here Mike was, twenty years old and suddenly possessing unusual amounts of time, money, and influence. He didn't have a rule book with easy answers. But he did have an ally.

When young players enter the NHL, they're required to live with someone. During Mike's first year he lived with a family in Ottawa. But during his second year,

Mike lived with his cousin Warren, who had moved to the area with his wife for a job. The timing was divine.

"Warren helped me with a lot of things—dealing with the pressures, trying to figure out your faith," Mike said. "He'd gone through some of the things I had, kind of like an older brother who could help me out. So that was helpful for me."[6]

Regular time with Warren gave Mike a safe, godly person to help work through it all. "It was tough," Mike admitted. "Dealing with the pressures of money, as a kid making choices with the party scene, things like that ... It just didn't fulfill me."[7]

"I wasn't focused on God," he realized. "It was all about me, me, me."[8] Maybe Mike's *gifts* were the center of his life instead of the *gift Giver*. "You think of the highlights like getting your first goal or your first win, and you think that's neat. But I know the most important thing for me is having my faith."[9]

Mike recognized God's presence, but he was missing out on something better. Forget "religion" and its requirements. Warren got him excited about his *relationship* with God. "I wanted to experience this God that we all hear about," he explained. "That's where it became real for me. I knew I had to have a relationship with God to fulfill that inner peace of knowing I'm living my purpose, doing what God created me to do."[10]

With his cousin's influence and insight, Mike was able to reflect, refocus, and regain balance in his life at this NHL level. "Sometimes it takes awhile to find a true and real faith, and it took me living through some things to understand it was so real."[11]

Mike remembered his parents' advice of keeping Jesus at the center of his life and owned it. "When you get older you have to make your own decisions, you have to learn for yourself what's important," he said. "And [my family] really helped influence me from an early age."[12]

6

Number 12 and Captain Video

2001–2002

As Mike grounded himself in faith, he could better navigate the pressure of the pros. His focus started with his relationship with God, not just the reality of him. "Day to day, I try to have my time with God. It doesn't always happen, but it is what I like to have happen."[1] And game to game, Mike's focus included prayer—remembering his blessings and *whom* they came from.

So when pressures built up, Mike's foundation was already in place. Then his training as an athlete helped keep his balance through the season both on and off the ice. "When you get into a routine of playing hockey, every game you treat it the same," he explained. "You want to go out and compete the best possible, regardless of the situation around you. And that's what you train to do. And not letting pressure affect you. It can be hard to do, but I think as a hockey player, it's all about focus and realizing the ultimate goal of winning championships. And that's parallel to your faith too, really. And what we're here for is to serve and honor God and that's kind of allowed me to do that in hockey as well, and realizing the whole goal and trying to give that pressure to God. He wants to take some of that pressure away from us and let us compete and have fun, and he enjoys seeing us do that."[2]

It didn't hurt, too, that another strong believer joined the team. Roger Neilson, former Peterborough coach and legendary hockey leader, became an assistant coach with the Ottawa Senators.

Neilson was credited as the first coach to use video-tape analysis to teach players. "Captain Video," as he was sometimes called, was also the first to use micro-phone headsets to communicate with assistant coaches. As an assistant with the Senators, Neilson spent time in the press box with the headset, which not too long ago was revolutionary.[3]

While Neilson's great impact on hockey was well known, his influence on Mike was perhaps quieter but just as great. Neilson loved the sport, modeled Christian faith, and demonstrated serious tenacity, particularly in the midst of his ongoing fight with cancer. He rarely had a bad word for anyone regardless of disagreement, and he wasn't shy in crediting his faith for helping him deal with hardship.[4]

As the season got going, Mike found his groove. For two months, he was consistently recognized by the hard-to-please Canadian press for his outstanding performances. After each game, three game "stars" are selected, usually by someone in the media. The player with the most for the month is presented with the Molson Cup. (Most teams also donate money to charity in the name of the winner.) Mike won the December Molson Cup and was the co-winner (with Senator Captain Daniel Alfredsson) for January.

By the end of the season, Mike's numbers reflected his hard work on the ice: four game-winners, sixth in the league with three short-handed goals, first-ever penalty shot goal, five games where he earned at least two points, and one cool contest between young stars during the All-Star Game #52.

In addition to the personal achievements, an unusual highlight of the year came in the last two games. In a move labeled "the classiest move in league history," head coach Jacques Martin allowed Roger Neilson behind the bench to coach his 999th and 1000th game.[5] For a shutout in Boston and a loss in Toronto, the Ottawa Senators followed the lead of the legend. In April 2002, Neilson became only the ninth person to reach that milestone.

Boosted by the emotion of the moment, the team was determined to go deep into the playoffs. An overtime loss, though, in the first game of the first round generated panicked media coverage of postseason plights. If memories of last year's surprising exit from the first round haunted the players, they couldn't dwell on it. Focus became as important as ever—focus on what was *ahead* of them. Shift by shift, period by period, the Sens

Ottawa Senators defenseman Shane Hnidy (34), right winger Martin Havlat (9), and center Mike Fisher celebrate the Senators game-tying goal during third-period NHL second-round playoff action against the Toronto Maple Leafs in Toronto on Saturday, May 4, 2002.

took over the series against Philadelphia. Ottawa won the next four games, including an overtime victory on the road that ended the series in five games. The Flyers scored only twice in four games.

Ottawa continued to look forward. In the first match against the Maple Leafs, they handed a stunned Toronto crowd a stinging 5–0 loss. But in game number two, the pain was all Ottawa's—a loss that came in triple overtime. The teams battled back and forth until Ottawa led the series three to two. One more victory to go.

Then Mike was dealt a double heartbreaker. An injured Fisher had to watch the last two games of the series from the sidelines. And the Sens lost them both.

"It was a very up-and-down year for me, for sure," Mike said. In fifty-eight games, he had twenty-four points. But he also missed twenty-four games with a shoulder injury alone. "I just wish I had more of a chance to play."[6]

In addition, Fisher and the Senators once again faced an earlier-than-expected end to their season, losing in the first round of the playoffs. Grounded in God, Mike worked hard to rehabilitate his body and get ready for next season, hoping to come back stronger than ever.

7

Fight the Good Fight, Keep the Faith

2002–2003

The next season everything came together for Mike, more or less — *more* games played, *less* injuries. Making the most of his health, Fisher demonstrated on ice the countless hours of prep and practice he had put in when crowds weren't around. All of his statistics — goals, assists, points, power-play markers, plus/minus rating — were the highest numbers of his career.

But the year wasn't without its heartbreak. Assistant coach Roger Neilson continued to battle a merciless cancer. The Senators felt an urgency to win a Cup for him.

Fueled by emotional determination and blessed by good health, Mike and his teammates went to work each shift, throwing good checks and digging the puck from the corners. And when instigators and hockey pests tried to get Ottawa off their game, Mike stood up for himself and for his teammates.

Early in the season, a Boston Bruin caught Fisher's linemate with a stick. So Mike defended his teammate with some blows that delivered a clear message: If you play dirty with one of us you play dirty will all of us. In December, a frustrated Carolina Hurricane player tried to get his team going by steamrolling Fisher and then standing over him in a challenge. (Maybe he didn't realize how much Mike liked a challenge.) At the end of a scuffle, they had settled it; number twelve held his own.

By the postseason, the Senators had fought their way to the best record in the league with 113 points, fifty-two wins to just twenty-one losses. For the first time since 1989, the President's Cup was in Canada.

Great accomplishments behind them, there was still plenty of work to do. In the first round of the playoffs, the Sens dropped the Islanders in five games. Next stop: Philadelphia.

Ottawa split the first four games with the Flyers. Although the series stood at 2–2, the Senators had been shut out in each of their losses. And you can't win if you can't bury the puck. Two days later they were able to find the back of the net—five times. And then they showed it was no fluke by doing it again.

After the hurdle of not being able to score, the Senators continued to steamroll, blasting pucks through the pipes ten times in two games. Dramatically and decisively, Ottawa went to the Eastern Conference Finals for the first time in franchise history.

Dave Sandford/Getty Images/NHLI

Mike Fisher (#12) of the Ottawa Senators moves the puck past John Madden (#11) of the New Jersey Devils in game one of the Eastern Conference Finals of the 2003 Stanley Cup playoffs at the Corel Centre on May 10, 2003, in Kanata, Canada. The Senators defeated the Devils 3–2.

The winner of the next series would earn the right to play in the Stanley Cup Finals. The Senators faced off against the New Jersey Devils. In game one, Ottawa scored twice in the first period. New Jersey scored twice in the second. The teams battled through the third period, but no one could score. The nail-biter went to OT, where it took Ottawa three minutes to score the win.

But after the tough victory of game one, they lost the next three—one at home and two more on the road. Another loss, no matter how hard fought, meant the end of the road. The team had to give it everything they had for sixty minutes. Ottawa scored first on a surprising short-handed goal, a second one at even strength, and once again on the power play. Ottawa won the home game 3–1 to send the series back to New Jersey.

In game six, the two teams battled through a scoreless first period. Pucks were shot, penalties were caught, and regulation time ran out with the score tied at one. New Jersey was intense, but Ottawa was playing for their lives. Emotional penalties spilled into a heated overtime and after fifteen minutes, the Sens got the puck in the net.

In the seventh game of the series, Ottawa scored, and New Jersey tied it up. Then New Jersey scored, and Ottawa tied it up. With two minutes remaining on the clock, New Jersey scored the final goal to abruptly end the intensity. Just like that, the Sens joined twenty-eight teams that also ended their season without hoisting the Stanley Cup.

While New Jersey went on to win the finals, the Senators went home, especially disappointed to lose a chance at a championship they wanted for Roger Neilson. At the same time, they knew a hard-fought series wasn't the same as the hard-fought battle that their assistant coach faced with cancer. Less than a month later, Roger's funeral was held in Peterborough.

"He was an inspiration for me," Mike said. "Just in the way he carried himself. He was always respectful of everyone, and he was just a likeable guy. He was funny, and at the same time he really spoke the truth, and he was very adamant about his faith and what was important to him."[1]

Neilson's example had reinforced what Mike's parents had demonstrated growing up—the importance of faith. God-given faith bears the weight of life's troubles and challenges. And it offers rewards that last forever. "Sometimes it's very humbling to realize that we are here today and gone tomorrow," Mike said. "I find true comfort in God's grace, knowing that I fall short in many ways, but he's always there for me through the good times and bad—no matter what."[2]

Neilson had affected the sport of hockey, but his impact extended way beyond the walls of the arena. Not only had Neilson touched the lives of those he worked with, but his legacy led to Roger's House—a place for families to stay when their children are sick in the hospital. Only the second one of its kind in Canada, it could accommodate treating kids with cancer and the families who support them. Right away Mike began serving as honorary chair.

Often a relationship with God can look like one with a new neighbor—it's nice to have him there but you're not going to share any secrets with him. It's not a bad place to start, but God wants a deeper relationship that includes sharing secrets, sharing time, sharing a bond.

Mike's relationship with God—his trust in him, his time with him—had been growing since he was young. He had considered getting baptized as a step of obedience but never made the move. "I always wanted to get baptized when I was younger but was timid in front of people so I put it off."

When he was twenty-three, Mike was pursuing God's invitation for a deeper relationship. "It's a part of who I am," he said, "and it has evolved the more I have matured and grown and experienced life."[3]

Wanting to be obedient and demonstrate his growing relationship with Christ, Mike was baptized at his church in Peterborough on August 24, 2003. "I decided to do it after Warren and I did our Bible study and when I decided it was time to get serious about my faith."[4]

"That's the most important decision you can make is following Christ," Mike said. "And there are ups and downs, many things that are difficult. But we're not alone. And Christ promises to help us if we give our lives to him ... Sometimes we try to change the outside first, but God wants us to change the inside. I've been through that. I've been through those struggles. When you can lay your trust in him, it's so exciting."[5]

8

The Arm Is Strong but It Ain't Straight

2003–2004

A natural result of hanging out with Christ every day is steady spiritual growth and wisdom—not just knowing biblical facts and stories but applying what you know. Knowledge is only the beginning. The heart plus prayer leads to real wisdom.

Although he lived in a hotbed of pressure and temptation that claims athletes and professionals every day, Mike showed unusual maturity and he demonstrated uncommon wisdom—like avoiding places that lead only to pain, letting the frustrations of living with impossible expectations be handled by God instead of in public, and leading with actions instead of merely talking a good talk.

Mike's growing godly wisdom also helped him handle hardships and keep his balance through setbacks. And he was in for a big one.

For a while, the bursa sac on Fisher's right elbow had been inflamed, swollen like a large golf ball. Time hadn't helped. In fact, the bursitis only got worse. Finally, surgery helped the swelling but weakened his arm.

So a couple months later in practice, when his arm was hit with a stick, a tendon near his bicep tore. The injury required more surgery, a couple of screws, and a lot of recovery time. It was supposed to take four to six weeks to heal, but it was taking longer.

Perhaps coaches were feeling the frustration of the injury too, because there was some question why the injury was taking so long to heal. Mike was taken aback. No one had ever questioned his drive or toughness. While he faced the familiar disappointing frustrations of not being able to play, not even being able to travel with the team, he had never before been doubted. It was a grim season.

During the unusual amount of time at home, Mike was hanging out with God, hanging out with his roommate, and just being himself. "The team was on the road. I was at home. We'd just finished watching the hockey game."[1] The friends were talking about everything, including setbacks, frustrations, and faith. And then, without planning or plotting, Mike's roommate became a believer.

"I think God gives you opportunities at certain times to speak the truth," he realized. "I think that's important for me, whenever there's an opportunity, to grab it and continue to make ourselves available."[2]

Mike's injury, the time away from the game, the disappointment, the doubt—none of it was wasted. "Right then I realized that's why everything happened. It was the most frustrating ..." he said, trailing off. "I actually doubted ever coming back at one point. Because I was supposed to be getting better and I wasn't, and then I got hurt again. But right when that happened and my friend [Mike's roommate] became a Christian and decided he wanted to have a faith and follow Jesus, I knew what God had been doing. And it made it that much better."[3] Mike took one for the team. And as hard as it was, it was worth it.

To this day, Mike can't straighten his arm because of the screws that healed the tendon above his elbow. But it's not a sore subject. It's a graphic reminder of the season where God caused everything to work together for good.

In March, Mike was finally back. With the playoffs just around the corner, the Senators faced the Flyers in a testy match in Philadelphia. By the third period, it got downright ugly.

With a few minutes to go and a few goals to make up, a Philly "enforcer" took on a Senator in a scrap (fight) that had to be broken up by the refs. As the two players were skating to the penalty box, the rest of the players on the ice—including the goalies, like padded sumo wrestlers—began to brawl. The ice looked like a yard sale of gloves, helmets, and sticks.

Even Mike got in on the action and faced off with 6' 4" Philly center Michal Handzus. The announcer watched the fight unfold and called it: "Handzus is much larger, but I like Fisher's chances here."[4] They spun and scrapped, and Mike dropped him twice before getting split up by the refs.

An unusually large-scale brawl left the refs with the unusually large-scale job of sorting out over four hundred minutes of penalties. It took them an hour-and-a-half. While Philadelphia logged 213 penalty minutes, Ottawa finished with 203 and six men left on the bench.

Hockey fans appreciated the intensity of giving it all on the ice, and they respected the honor of teammates who had each others' backs. Sports writers who watched hockey for a living appreciated it too. In April, Mike was selected by the Ottawa chapter of the Professional Hockey Writers Association for the Masterton Award. The Bill Masterton Memorial Trophy is given every year to the pro player who best shows perseverance, sportsmanship, and dedication to hockey.

"It's a real honor to get nominated for an award like this," Mike said at the time. "This has been a tough year for me."[5]

Romans 12:12— "Be glad for all God is planning for you. Be patient in trouble, and always be prayerful."

Throughout the season, Mike had played only twenty-four games, the least in his entire career. Watching sixty

Jim Young/Reuters/Landov

Mike Fisher of the Ottawa Senators scores the game-winning goal past Toronto Maple Leafs goaltender Ed Belfour during the second overtime period in Game 6 of their NHL Eastern Conference quarterfinal in Ottawa, April 18, 2004. The Senators defeated the Leafs 2–1 to even the series at three games each.

games from the sidelines is tough for any player who loves to compete. But facing hardships and trouble, he continued to work hard to be in game-shape and keep a positive attitude, knowing God was in control. "When you go through some of the things that I've gone through, it's not easy. There are things that you don't expect to happen and that makes it tough. I wasn't really sure (about playing this year.) I didn't know what was going to happen. It's great to be back."[6]

Going into the playoffs, Ottawa faced the Maple Leafs in Toronto's building—a drawback that didn't slow the Sens down during the first game. They won 4–2. But by the fifth game, the Sens had been shut out three times.

Ottawa faced elimination in the sixth game. The Sens lost the lead early. Finally they got one goal by Toronto to force overtime. The teams traded shots and checks through the first OT, but nobody could score. Then, only one minute forty-six seconds into the second overtime, Mike took a cross-crease pass and rifled a wrist shot to the back of the net.

"We had a lot to prove, especially after game five," he said. "It was obviously big, one of the biggest goals I've scored, but it was a whole-team effort. I was lucky to get a bounce in front and bury it."[7]

The Senators had forced a seventh game with hard-nosed hockey. Ultimately, the intensity might have been too hard to sustain. Ottawa's goalie, who had stopped an outstanding forty-five shots in game six, let three shots out of eleven get by in game seven. That's a tough blow to recover from. The Sens were done.

After eight years and eight playoff appearances, coach Jacques Martin was fired. And the National Hockey League was preparing for a labor dispute that would last almost one full year. Mike would need wisdom and faith as he headed into the uncertainty and leaned on God.

9

Raise Your Sticks and Smack the Glass

2004–2005

After the summer, all play in the National Hockey League froze like a wet sweater in a windy blizzard while team owners and the players' union figured out what to do with the league's earnings. There were no simple solutions or compromises, so until they could agree about what to do with profits—until the labor dispute was resolved—none of the thirty teams would play.

Because lockout rumors had rumbled all summer, Mike knew the season might be delayed. In September, it became official. The 2004–2005 season would be postponed until a settlement was reached. Like a lot of players, Mike stayed in game-shape and waited. As soon as the owners and players' union could agree to terms, the season would get underway.

But the weeks ticked by, and the window for the season got smaller and smaller. Mike continued to work out on his own, but by October he knew he had to do something different. He didn't want to take a year off, and he didn't want to go down to the minor league system like some other players. Nearly four hundred professional hockey players went to the European leagues for the season. So when Mike's agent came to him with a chance to play there, Mike decided to go. He packed up to play for EV Zug of the top Swiss National League.

Mike was no longer a drive away from family, no longer speaking the predominant language, no longer known by his teammates. "It was different being on my own a little bit, but I got to meet some good people too."[1] Both of his coaches were Canadian, so that made it a little easier and more familiar.

And of course, he was glad to be playing—although even the hockey was a little different. The ice surface was fifteen feet wider so the game was more open with more time on the puck. It didn't take long for him to adjust his style to the extra time it allowed to make plays. The league was even more competitive than Mike thought, which suited him perfectly, and he settled into the game well. (Mike scored 9 goals and had 18 assists for 27 points in twenty-one games.)

The biggest difference Mike noticed had less to do with the game and everything to do with the wild fans packing the small arena. In the NHL, huge arenas carry a variety of fans—families, casual observers, die-hards. But the fans generally don't carry sparklers like they do in Switzerland or repeat chants better left untranslated. "The fans there are nuts, like *nuts*. They're *passionate* fans—which was fun."[2]

Mike had been playing hockey for a lot of years, but he had never seen anything like the post-game parties. After a win, the team gathered at center ice and faced the crazy crowd at the end of the rink. The players held their sticks, then raised them up slowly as they skated toward the crowd that grew louder and louder. When the players got to the end boards, they smacked the glass, and the fans went into a frenzy, like they had flaming sparklers in their pockets.

"The first time," Mike laughed, "I was like, *what are we doing?*"[3]

Another surprise came in one of the first games Mike played with the EV Zug. The announcer named Fisher as the player of the game. The crowd started chanting his name. He remembered trying to communicate over the noise. "And all the guys were saying, 'You gotta go back! You gotta go back!' And I was like, *'For what?'*"[4]

But Mike obliged, starting at center by himself and skating toward the crowd—lifting his stick, smacking the glass. His new fans went wild!

Between the competitions and the celebrations, Mike kept his eye on Ottawa. Along with every other hockey player and fan, Mike hoped the NHL season would get underway. In January, the league made a last-ditch effort to save the season, but the parties couldn't resolve their differences. For the first time ever, a major pro sports league in North America cancelled a complete season because of a labor dispute. For the first time since 1919, no names were engraved on Lord Stanley's Cup. Mike set out to make the most of the opportunity. "It was kind of the year of something different I knew I might not ever get to experience again."[5] He moved out of the hotel where he was staying and moved in with a teammate. And along with exhibition games in different countries like Latvia and Germany, Fish took advantage of breaks in the game schedule to explore Europe. His sister came to visit and together they drove to Venice. His friend came over and together they checked out London.

During weekends off, Mike explored the surrounding mountains, blue lakes, and distinctive countryside. Getting outside and listening to good worship music always made it easy for him to reflect on all God had made and done. "When I was in Europe I was listening to Shawn McDonald," Mike remembered. "Every time I hear his first CD now, I always think of Switzerland because I would listen to that CD nonstop."[6]

He also tracked down a church in Zurich he'd heard about. About a half hour away, International Christian Fellowship (ICF) encouraged everyone to learn about Christ. "I'd pick up the English headphones because everything was in Swiss German." In a beautiful building in Switzerland, a big, diverse congregation with a special Canadian guest came together to worship God.

But it didn't take a church to remind him of the truth he already knew. If God was the center of his life, everything else would work out—including his career. In

July, after a 310-day lockout, the NHL was ready to roll. So was Mike.

After the playoffs with EV Zug and before he returned to Canada, Mike experienced another part of Europe, this time with a bunch of his countrymen. He joined Team Canada for the World Championships. For two weeks in May, he enjoyed being a gritty presence with fellow pros he hadn't seen in a full season.

Some hometown visitors got to enjoy it too — Mike's parents, older brother, and some buddies had missed his play for long enough and went overseas to cheer on Canada.

Sixteen national teams trekked to Austria to compete in the international competition. In the first round in Innsbruck, Team Canada scored seventeen goals (the most of all the teams) and was scored *on* only five times.

In the next round, they played three games in four days and skated away with a win, a loss, and a tie. Most importantly, Team Canada qualified for the next stage. In the quarterfinals, they were tied with Slovakia after two periods (with an assist from Fish). In a nail-biting third period, Canada scored two, Slovakia scored one. On to the semifinals!

They played a tough Team Russia where the game summary read like a rap sheet: slashing, elbowing, tripping, roughing, boarding, unsportsmanlike conduct, checking to the head. Canada hammered in four goals in the first two

Mike with his parents, Karen and Jim, at the Niesen Mountain in Switzerland, 2009, when Mike had returned again to Europe to play for Team Canada in the IIHF World Championship.

periods, then watched Russia get to within one goal before time ran out. Team Canada had made it to the finals!

In the championship in Vienna, the Czech Republic held a slim one-point lead through the first two periods. And they apparently built a wall in front of the net, because Canada couldn't score. On May 15, a 3–0 loss earned Team Canada a silver medal.

Because of the unfortunate, interfering, and difficult lockout, Mike experienced interesting, beautiful, and unique Europe. With the end of his worshipful and memorable stay, Mike was ready to get back onto the ice in Ottawa.

10

12:12

2005–2006

For two seasons in a row, Mike played less than thirty games. A pro player can play triple that in one season. But he trained to stay sharp mentally and strong physically. "We have a workout program that our trainer gives us which consists of weights, plyometrics, running, biking, and lots of other fun stuff," he offered. "I enjoy doing my workouts outside so I try to do that as much as I can."[1]

"I have had to cut back on desserts a lot ... and that's hard because my mom bakes all the time," he said. "I've paid more attention to nutrition over the last couple of years. It's like fuel in a car. The better the octane, the better performance you're going to get from your body."[2]

Over the summer, he spent extra time improving his footwork and core strength that helped his speed on the ice. "Speed is the biggest part of my game . . . and it's the way the game is going," he said.[3] Rule changes and enforced obstruction penalties—no more holding, hooking, or interference allowed—would help his offensive play. "I think I've been able to use my speed in the new style of the NHL and it's helped my game," he said.[4]

As always, Mike approached the season with determination and focus. Distractions like reporters, rumors, and trades could be overwhelming if you let it get to you. He could either focus on the distractions or focus on his game. And focus could be the difference between putting the puck in the net and fanning on it.

"You can get caught up trying to figure out where you fit in instead of worrying about playing your best and letting those things take care of themselves," said Mike. "Just go out and stick to the best part of your game and bring that every night regardless of who you're playing with. If you do that, that's all you can worry about."[5]

So this seven-year pro focused on improving. "Competing and trying to be better as a player—because I'm a very competitive player—really motivates me."[6]

Off the ice, he kept his focus as well. "In life, trying to honor God and trying to serve him is a big part in what motivates me to play too," Mike said. "Because I know he's given me this talent, this ability, and I'm very honored and blessed to have that and I'm going to try and give back everything I can toward him because he's been gracious to me. That motivates me to be not just a great player, but being the best person I can, because of what he's done for me in my life and ultimately on the cross."[7]

After returning from the lockout, Mike recorded more than forty points each year for three straight years. The rule changes plus Mike's determination and training resulted in improvement, even for a veteran—which was good, because Ottawa wasn't reaching simply for a post-season appearance. It was going for the Cup.

The Senators steamrolled through their first twenty-five games, earning a win on twenty-one of them. Preseason as well as playoffs, goals and grit, Mike made an impact on all corners of the ice. During one shift against the traditional provincial rival Toronto, Mike won the face-off, endured a hit from the Leafs' Darcy Tucker (who ricocheted to the ice), shot on goal, followed another shot, thumped another defender to the ice, and chased the puck to the boards. Apparently Tucker hadn't taken too kindly to bouncing off Mike like a tennis ball, so he followed Mike around the ice trying to catch up. Instead of going to the bench, he wanted to argue with his gloves off. And so they did. Mike finished his long shift without ever leaving his feet—and Tucker was lying on the ice again.

Averaging nearly four goals per game, the Sens ended December with the best record in the NHL.

In the dog days of the season, Ottawa sagged some. The Olympics disrupted their momentum and the

Senators' veteran goalie hurt his back. But unless the wheels came off, they were still on track.

In March, they headed to Boston, who were on a skid of their own. The Bruins had topped the Sens in the previous meeting that season, and this would be a close match. But worse than losing points to a defeat, they lost Fisher.

In an aggressive penalty kill, Mike drove up the ice with the puck and quickly slid into the boards, where his ankle got caught and twisted. He tried to skate off but went back to his knees, as a stab of pain tore through his weak ankle.

As he was helped off the ice, his mind swirled: *hurt again ... end of the season ... playoffs just around the corner ... a broken ankle will take forever to heal ... we're playing so well ...*

And then Mike noticed the time clock — 12:12. The competitive athlete was reminded of the eternal perspective: the God who loved him was in control.

The Sens lost to the Bruins in a shootout. But they also got good news. An MRI showed that Mike's injury wasn't as serious as everyone expected — no break, no ligament damage. He needed time to recover, of course, but he would be back for the playoffs.

"The feeling is this is something we can be positive about," Mike said to anxious reporters at the time. "The sooner I can get back, the better, but it would have been a lot worse it if was a break. There's no question."[8]

"I really think we caught a break," said Ottawa's General Manager John Muckler, "because he didn't break his ankle and I really thought he had when I saw the way he went into the boards and saw the replays. I was really worried that we were going to be without him for a while."[9]

SensNation breathed a collective sigh of relief. Blogs fired up. Reporters weighed in. Fans did independent research on medical terminology and degrees of sprains to calculate if Mike could be ready for the playoffs in five weeks.

Mike returned to the ice in two weeks.

Romans 12:12 remained in Mike's mind — and on his stick. Now before games, he would write the Bible reference right on the grip. "It's just kind of a reminder," he explained, "that God's got a perfect plan for you and just be patient because trouble is going to arise and have that faith in him and always be in prayer."[10]

Mike set personal bests with a plus/minus rating of +23, 149 shots on goal, and a shooting percentage of more than 14 percent. The Senators finished the regular season at the top of the Eastern Conference (52 – 21 – 9). They led the league with the most goals (312), the most shorthanded goals (25), and the most shots on goal (2,811).

The Ottawa Senators were clicking as a team and feeling the sweet success of working together. "We're playing well, we're having a lot of fun as a team," said Mike. "The city's been buzzing. The fans have been great. Playoff time's the best."[11]

In the first round, the Senators were favored against the Tampa Bay Lightning. The teams split the first two

games in Ottawa. In the third game, Mike took a puck
to his face when he was caught in the way as a linemate was trying to clear the puck. A trip to the hospital
showed a fracture below his right eye. Can't mess with

Photo provided by Jim and Karen Fisher

Further proof Mike loves to hike, fish, and spend time outdoors
with his family. Here he and his sister Meredith are in Switzerland,
2004.

the orbital bone. And can't miss the playoffs. So Mike went with something he hadn't worn since his peewee-league days — the face cage. He was back in the lineup for games four and five to help eliminate the Lightning.

The Senators would need everyone for the next round against their divisional rivals, the Buffalo Sabres. Gritty players on both squads meant a hard-core series between the first and second teams in the Northeast Division.

Game one was an indication of what was to come. The Sens held the lead as the final moments ticked away. But with eleven seconds left in the game, Buffalo sent it into overtime — and then scored the game-winner in the high-scoring 7–6 stunner.

Even though the Sens allowed only seventeen shots in game two, they still walked away with the loss. They won game three but lost two more OT heartbreakers and were out in five games.

With dignity and composure, Mike faced the local news station. "Obviously we're all disappointed that we couldn't do better. You know we've got a lot of time to think about it and get revved up for next year."[12]

A painful end to a good season meant more work for the Senators next season. Mike's health and focus (regardless of distractions) gave him a strong season that helped his team. His individual efforts weren't ignored. While posting forty-four points in the offensive zone, he was also recognized for his strong defense by earning a nomination for the Selke Trophy. Honoring two-way play, the Frank J. Selke Trophy goes to the best defensive forward in the league.

Next year, Mike wanted nothing more than his individual offensive and defensive efforts to help his team win the Cup.

Mike used the summer to relax and rest his body. Apparently for Mike, *relaxation* meant hiking, and *rest* meant carrying a canoe over his head. He went up to Ontario's vast, natural Algonquin Park with his brother Rob and his cousins Warren and Lloyd (Warren's brother). Together, they "relaxed" and "rested" like crazy.

Surrounded by wilderness that covers more land than the state of Delaware, the group explored areas accessible only by hiking or paddling. With canoes over their heads, they trekked from lake to lake to row, explore, and catch something to eat.

At one impasse, the kindred daredevils jumped into the water from sixty feet. (Don't try this at home!) After hitting the water, Rob bruised his tailbone. Warren hurt his feet from the impact. At least Mike could walk. "I forgot to tuck my hands in," he said. "My hands slapped [the water], and they went numb."[13]

Canoeing and portaging around the lakes and trails of the untamed park did his spirit good. He got a rare chance to spend long amounts of time with the guys. He enjoyed uninterrupted time to reflect on how big and how good God is. Outside with close family, he came away humbled and happy—and yes, relaxed and rested.

11

The Senators and Lord Stanley

2006–2007

Ottawa skated into the new season with a record that was ... entirely disappointing. By December, the mighty Sens had lost as many as they had won with a record of 17–18–1. To make matters worse, Mike missed fourteen games in December due to a knee injury.

Despite the demoralizing record, they fought back to make it into the playoff picture. "Obviously we had a tough start," said Mike. "But when Jason Spezza, myself, and Antoine Vermette went out, the guys really picked it up and played unbelievable ... We learned how to win and really had to work hard, and we became a team then."[1]

By Valentine's Day, Fish was back in fighting shape. Good timing, because the Florida Panthers weren't feeling the love for the Sens. When Panthers' center Chris Gratton hit the back of Mike's knee, it was go time. Mike spent the first few seconds ducking fists and trying to get his visor off. ("Just being nice, I guess,"[2] he grinned.) When Fish finally engaged, he had a reach disadvantage but pushed the Panther up against the boards and switched hands. After thirty long seconds, the linesmen moved in. In the second period, Mike scored, and the Sens shut them out 4–0. Happy Valentine's Day.

With their victory, the Sens safeguarded a five-game winning streak. The team headed north from Florida to Buffalo—and got no love there either. A frosty rivalry had started in the last series, and the chill hadn't faded. In fact, it might have gotten a little cooler.

In the second period, when Buffalo's captain snapped a shot, a Senator hit him hard, sending his helmet flying and taking the captain out of the game. The Sabres retaliated at the next face-off with a fighting fourth-line player targeting a skilled Senator. Neither team was going to warm up to each other any time soon.

All twelve players paused the game to air out their differences. The result was one hundred minutes of penalties.

And still, a game had to be played. With nine minutes left, Mike tied the score to send the game into overtime. Five minutes later, the teams entered a shootout. Six shots later, the score was still tied. Finally, a backhander flipped in—for Buffalo. Reminiscent of the previous playoff series, Buffalo won 6–5. The bitter rivalry between the two top teams in the Northeast Division continued.

For the second year in a row, Mike set personal bests—48 points and 26 assists. The Sens ended the regular season with a record of 48 wins, 25 losses, and 105 points. The only team with more points in their division was Buffalo.

Before the playoffs got underway, a memorable team practice was invaded by an angel-faced, mini Senator. A three-year-old named Elgin Fraser had been battling terminal cancer. Thanks to the Children's Wish Foundation, arrangements were made for Elgin to gear up and come out onto the ice. In an Ottawa uniform, he got to skate around the ice in Mike's arms.

"His parents said he always liked to go fast, so I wheeled him around. The faster you went, the more excited he got," Mike said. "We all had a really good time with him."[3]

Elgin and his family were touched by all the players, and the athletes were also moved by Elgin. Like many kids, he needed the specialized help of Roger's House—the legacy of Neilson and a cause Mike continued to support. "I feel very fortunate and blessed to be able to do what I do," Fisher admitted. "In the spotlight, I just want to give back where I can and help others. There's nothing better than when I can help a little kid or see the difference you can make."[4]

Elgin-Alexander Fraser takes a twirl with Mike Fisher around Scotiabank Place ice.

If he was blessed with determination, drive, and skill, it wasn't just to perform well or only to win the Stanley Cup. His blessings reached way off the ice. Mike knew that his familiar face and position in the community allowed him a distinctive opportunity to make a difference. Attention from a hockey star can brighten someone's day with a memory that will last forever, even if it can't take their illness away. "I love doing it whenever I can. It's a lot of fun—and hard too at the same time."[5]

When the playoffs started in April, Ottawa went out faster than Fisher's 105-mph slap shot. In the first series, they beat a young Pittsburgh team in five games. In the second series, they beat an experienced New Jersey team in five games as well.

In the Eastern Conference Finals, the Sens faced embittered rivals in Buffalo. Staring down each others' full playoff beards (players stop shaving until their team gets eliminated or wins the Stanley Cup), each team knew what was at stake.

Mike scored first on a strong, short-handed breakaway, but after two periods the teams were tied. With patience and confidence, Ottawa scored three goals in the third period to win the first game.

In the second game, Buffalo wanted to bury the Sens. And the Sens had to climb out of a two-goal hole. First, Captain Daniel Alfredsson scored, and then Mike scored to tie up the game. Both teams hung on through two tough overtimes when Ottawa finally got a bounce. It was the first time in franchise history that the Senators won the first two games of a playoff series.

Game three was a well-fought, one-goal win. But they lost game four at home, sending the series back to Buffalo.

In Ottawa, Elgin and his family had been cheering with the rest of SensNation. Between games four and five, Mike quietly visited him at home. "I was hanging out with him and he asked me if we were going to win the Cup," Mike said. "It was something that I was glad and very thankful that I was able to do."[6] Mike said good-bye and left for game five in Buffalo.

The first period was tied at zero. By the end of the third period, the game was tied again at two goals apiece. Then nine minutes into OT, Ottawa's captain scored. You could have heard a puck drop in the arena.

All the cheering and shouting was three hundred miles away in Ottawa.

The Senators were going to the Stanley Cup Finals!

Mike credited the team for working together. "If we can make sure we're good defensively, it creates chances the other way," he said of his line that dominated Buffalo's second line. "We're chipping in with some big goals and so have some of the other lines."[7]

But some tough news dampened the celebration. The team found out that Elgin's cancer became too much, and the young boy had died after the Sens defeated Buffalo on the road. "The impact he had on me was incredible," Mike admitted at the time. "With the things he went through and how well he handled them, I was blessed to spend some time with him."[8] Mike and teammate Chris Phillips served as pallbearers at Elgin's funeral.

The tough task of shifting their focus to their jobs on the ice tested each professional on the team. The Finals still had to be played. Ottawa waited for the western conference to finish their series. They had nine days to rest and try to maintain playoff intensity and focus.

In game one, Mike took the puck and scored, effectively introducing the Sens to Anaheim. Recent history showed that when Ottawa scored first, they would win. But this time, the Sens couldn't keep the lead and they lost a close contest 3 to 2.

In game number two, only one puck went into the net—for Anaheim. Down two games to none, Ottawa looked forward to challenging the Anaheim Ducks at home.

Fisher (#12) of the Ottawa Senators skates after the puck under pressure from Chris Pronger (#25) of the Anaheim Ducks during game one of the 2007 Stanley Cup finals on May 28, 2007, at the Honda Center in Anaheim, California.

June 2, 2007, marked the first Stanley Cup playoff game in Canada's capital city in eighty years. SensNation was as pumped as the players. In a hard-charging, electrifying match, the Sens came from behind three times, including a tip-in from Fish on the point.

Both teams refused to give up. When Mike saw his teammate get popped from behind along the boards, he charged in to help. Fish pulled Anaheim's Ryan Getzlaf away and wrestled him to the ice. Holding him down with his left forearm, his bare right hand on Getzlaf's shoulder, they talked nose-to-nose. Despite being on top, his opponent having no defense, Mike declined to give the Duck a face wash or a shot to the chin.

Here's what the announcer saw: "Ryan Getzlaf's going to get the initial call because he goes in from behind ... Mike Fisher knows his role as a leader ... That's Mike Fisher being a gentleman. He could have come across with the right hand. Instead he doesn't. You know they talk about the code? There's the code—Fisher not taking advantage of Getzlaf being down on the ice in a prone position."[9]

Buoyed by the thunderous support of the rowdy crowd, the Senators enjoyed a 5–3 win at home.

"We know Mike is a hardworking, real determined type of guy with lots of character," said Coach Murray at the time. "His skating allows him to do an awful lot for us. Probably if you rate him over the three games, he was probably the best to this point."[10]

Mike's fire and fierce resolve stood out on the ice. Asked where his determination came from, Mike didn't hesitate. "I think my determination and work ethic is a gift, and I try to use all of my abilities for God's glory. That is my focus."[11]

"I think he's been probably our best forward in this series," said Captain Daniel Alfredsson. "He thrives on this kind of game—physical, fast-paced—and he's so strong, he's so quick, and I think the biggest thing is he has so much energy. He can go back, shift after shift, and play the way he does."[12]

Despite the heart, the teamwork, and goals from nine different Senators in the playoffs, Ottawa lost to Anaheim in five games. The Stanley Cup headed west, away from the capital city. For a nation that had gone more than a decade without winning "their" cup, after three straight chances this was a hard loss.

After the 102 games of the 2006–2007 season, Mike was spent physically and emotionally. He was ready to rest.

"When you get that close, there's disappointment because you don't know when you'll ever get that chance again," he admitted. "At the same time, I knew it wasn't meant to be, wasn't our year. We were still proud about what we'd done. So there was disappointment but still some satisfaction because of the process of getting there."[13]

They had left it all on the ice, gelled as a team, worked at common goals with uncommon success, and pushed the competition higher. With or without the Cup, the ride had been awesome.

By August 2007, Fish had gotten some rest. His bumps and bruises and banged-up body had healed (for the most part). His friend Tim Burke, who oversees all the NHL chapels through Hockey Ministries, had given Mike a book about the wilds of Alaska. After reading the adventures of the author/guide, Fish had only one response: "We've got to go!"

So Mike, Burke, Bud, and Warren flew to Anchorage. There, they hopped a flight to Red Devil and then to base camp. "The planes just kept getting smaller," he grinned.

While the other guys stayed at camp to fish, Mike split off with a guide to hunt for grizzlies — which meant another tiny plane. "We were getting low," he described, "and I was like, 'Uh, where are we landing?'" Apparently, the bank of a river was all they needed. For three days, Mike and the guide paddled the river with all their gear in a dinghy, looking for bear.

The Alaskan wild impressed even this seasoned outdoorsman. "You see pictures and video of Alaska, none of them do it justice," Mike said. "You have to experience it." With only two tiny humans for long, limitless miles, he took it all in, savoring the adventure of fishing, pitching a tent, and trekking along the river.

"One second we'd be in T-shirts, and then the storm would be moving in, and we'd be throwin' on the coat," he said smiling. "They say if you don't like the weather in Alaska, just wait fifteen minutes."

Before Mike went back with his group to fish for a few more days, he finally saw the awesome animal. It had been a worthwhile adventure whether or not he spotted any grizzlies. But on his last hunting day, Fisher saw seven. One of them now stands in his cottage near Peterborough.

The time on his own, with family, and with God, in this wide, wild place was just the retreat Mike needed. "I just like being outside," he said. "Hunting is an escape for me. It's just a good thinking time. It's a prayer time." And it's a memory that will last a lifetime.

12

Scores and Scraps

2007–2008

Over the summer, the Senators' front office had been working on a deal to keep Mike in Ottawa. During seven seasons, he recorded 92 goals, 100 assists, and 314 penalty minutes. And he contributed countless intangibles that couldn't be measured in a small box on the sports page—a selfless team player, a positive leader, a tough competitor with heart. Hard things to measure, but decision makers in the front office thought these qualities were worth a new contract.

"I was definitely thrilled that the team wanted to get something done," Mike said. "I couldn't see myself playing anywhere else. The team showed a lot of confidence in me. I'm really blessed for sure."[1]

While slumps threaten focus, success can be just as damaging a distraction. Read the good press, care about statistics more than the team, and it gets easier to believe that a significant salary is well deserved. But Mike knew that as a servant of God, he didn't do things on his own, and it was never *all about him.*

As opinion and coverage centered on his new contract, Mike focused on his game and on God. "Playing hockey in the NHL has been a dream of mine since I was young, and realizing this dream at the age of nineteen was an unbelievable experience for me," he admitted. "It's hard for me to describe how lucky I feel to be playing the game I love. I am very fortunate to be able to make a living playing hockey, but I have come to realize that playing in the NHL is only a small part of who I am and not the part that defines me. Having a personal relationship with Jesus Christ is what I believe truly defines a person and how we find eternal significance."[2]

Be glad for all God is planning for you. Be patient in trouble, and always be prayerful. With Romans 12:12 written on the handle of his stick, Mike went to work.

During the first part of the season, the Senators lit up the scoreboard by winning an impressive eight games in a row. Mike's north-south game helped keep the team going in a winning direction.

When the Sens played the Carolina Hurricanes in December, Mike scored in an offensive push. And then he played tough defense that demonstrated another aspect of hockey. Big-time brawler Stu Grimson, who started playing in the NHL in the late '80s, explained it this way: "A fighter is a protector and, if you're a Christian as I am, who better to protect someone than a Christian."[3]

So against Carolina, Fisher took on the role of protector when his goalie was hit by the other team. The puck was cleared, but Mike beelined for the offending forward to stick up for his netminder. The other player took a swipe, and Mike dropped his gloves for a hard-hitting battle along the boards. Finally, the linesmen moved in to break it up. The Hurricane player took the opportunity for two last cheap shots: a headbutt to Mike's face and another left jab around the linesman.

Carolina had to play shorthanded when the player received goalie interference and an attempt to injure. So the headbutt cost his team. It also cost Mike a tooth. "It didn't come out right away," he said. "It was just loose because it broke high at the top, and they couldn't save it."[4] The Senators shut down the Hurricanes 6–0.

While he waited to get a new tooth set, Mike also suffered an injury to his core. By the end of December though, he returned to the ice to get three more goals — in *one* game. Hat trick! "Eight years coming," he laughed, "but it feels good."[5]

Despite a strong start, the Sens fell into a slump. After the team won only seven of twenty-one games, head coach John Paddock was fired. But their record (43–31–8) ended up qualifying them for the playoffs — barely.

Although Mike played a career-high seventy-nine games, a knee injury ended his season right before the postseason. The Sens were swept in the first round.

"Sometimes, even this year, you go through struggles on the ice, and it [helps] just to keep things focused on God," Mike said. "Things seem to make a little more sense."[6]

Mike's summer schedule allowed him to pursue interests he couldn't during the season. Ottawa's club and team leaders set a worthy example with community work and charity. Mike felt he could take on even more.

"It's humbling," Mike explained. "You've really got to give everything to God, because everything I have is really his, and he's given me the opportunity to play at this level, and with that comes a lot of responsibility too."[7]

He didn't have to be a missionary or pastor to serve God. He could serve in a way that was uniquely suited to Mike and his gifts. So Fisher initiated something that would help young hockey players *and* local charities. He started a summer hockey school.

Largely because of his stature in Ottawa, the Mike Fisher Hockey Camp drew young players who wanted to learn from the pros and compete for the cup (the Roger Neilson Cup, affectionately named for the local legend). Counselors helped them develop their game but also

Mike instructing young players at his hockey camp.

have fun—just like Mike was encouraged when he was a young player.

"I want them to obviously get better as a hockey player and come and have fun and meet a lot of good people which I did as a kid," he explained. "Just as important off the ice, I want them to learn about being a good person and growing and learning from the game, learn a lot of different life skills too. Seeing the kids, having other players from the team come in, seeing the excitement, watching them have fun—it's pretty neat."[8]

Just as important, 100 percent of the proceeds that were raised with the summer camp sessions went to charities like Roger's House and the regional Make-a-Wish Foundation. That way the Mike Fisher Hockey Camp could help a lot more kids than just healthy skaters and hockey fans. "To be able to have the charity aspect, and know that a lot of other kids are going to benefit from it, it's kind of a win-win."[9]

When his parents were shuttling him to rinks, Mike might have had only hockey on his mind. He was just showing up to play with a puck. But his gifts for hockey along with his heart to follow God led him way beyond the rink. If he defined himself as a hockey player, he would have stayed on the ice. But because Fisher defined himself first as a man of faith, he has looked to go outside the ice, to trumpet his faith, to partner with people who help kids, and to influence people with his actions even more than his words.

13

I'll Play Anywhere

2008–2009

Going into the 2008–2009 season, it seemed like Mike pretty much had it made. He'd realized his dream of playing in the big leagues when he was still in his teens. He'd been a pro for nearly ten years. The experienced veteran had a guaranteed contract, was a well-liked teammate, adored by fans ... What else could he learn?

For any successful athlete, it's easy to get wrapped up in entitlements—thinking that he *earned* a certain status on his team and *deserved* certain things on the ice. But instead of seeing things as rights, Mike still saw them as gifts. The Bible says that God is in control and all good things come from him. And frankly, Mike believed God. When you think things are about God, not about you, you don't have to convince yourself to be humble.

So when he was bombarded with questions and scenarios by the media— *You're a center, but you might have to play on the wing . . . What if you get put on a third or fourth line? . . .* Mike didn't even pause to think about an answer. "I'll play anywhere," Mike replied easily.

"I just want to be a big part of this team," he said. "I know I'm going to get a lot of opportunity to play big minutes in a lot of situations, so I want to step in and contribute offensively and be a tough player to play against, to do everything and more than I've done in the past."[1]

His lack of ego, his concern for the team more than for his own stats, and his God-given competitive drive made him valuable on the ice and in the locker room. "(Fisher) brings a little bit of everything," Sens new head coach Craig Hartsburg said. "He's very intense and he's got great speed, he can shoot the puck and he's good at both ends of the rink. He adds a lot to your hockey team . . . Fisher has a lot of assets."[2]

His assets would be needed, because the Senators were in for a year that would be tougher than slapping a pea through a Cheerio—changes in lineups, changes in coaches (their fourth in a year), low number of goals, high number of losses.

Despite the slumps and disappointing numbers, the team fought for each other. As a nod to solidarity and a tangible reminder to shore up, they decided to grow mustaches (a lot like playoff beards).

During that stretch of time, Mike defended his captain in a blatant show of protection. In Buffalo, an aggressive

Sabre clipped linemate Alfredsson in the neutral zone. Blazing up the ice to get ready for a pass, Mike skated by the play and abruptly U-turned to remind the Sabre that no one clips the captain.

Despite the team's best efforts, they couldn't change the momentum enough to qualify for the playoffs. For the first time since 1996, the Senators' season ended in April.

At the end of the month, Mike revisited his old digs in Europe. The World Championships were in Switzerland, where Fisher had played during the NHL lockout. Now Mike was playing for Team Canada in an arena only twenty miles (31 km) from the crowd that had greeted him with chants and sparklers.

In the first round Team Canada dominated their three games by scoring a sensational twenty-two goals. Mike got in on the action with three points.

In the next round, Team Canada ran over the Czech Republic to win 5–1. And then they did the same thing to Norway. But in the next game, Team Canada found themselves trailing. For two periods Finland maintained an early lead. Mike provided a tough presence on the ice for nearly nineteen minutes, and finally Canada tied it up halfway through the third to force the OT. But when neither team could score, the game was decided by a shootout. Canada recorded their first loss but still qualified for the next round.

In the quarterfinals in Bern, Switzerland, Canada faced off against Latvia. For the first twenty minutes the teams traded penalties and shots, but no one could bury the puck. In the next period Canada took the lead and never gave it up.

Canada played the semifinal game against Sweden in front of more than 11,000 hockey fans. Mike was on the ice for more than twenty gritty minutes. Canada scored in the first period and twice in the second period (with an assist from Fish). When the last minutes ticked off, they knew they were in the finals of the World Championships.

In a rematch of the 2008 World Championship Finals, Canada played Russia in a contest marked by its intensity. "It [is] like a playoff game," said a Russian forward. "Instead of best-of-seven, it's best-of-one."[3]

Canada scored early but seven minutes later Russia tied it up. With different playing styles and matching passion, the two teams battled back and forth. Russia recorded only seventeen shots on goal to Canada's thirty-eight. But by the end of regulation Russia also had two goals to Canada's one. Russia took gold. "We're not down because of the way we played," admitted the Canadian goalkeeper. "We are down because of the result of the game."[4]

In nine games with Team Canada, Mike had two goals, three assists, and a silver medal.

Mike used the summer months to rest up, spend time with people who weren't wearing skates, and do some work in the community, especially with his hockey school. His dad, his brother Bud, and a dedicated team of coordinators and counselors helped Mike improve and grow the camp.

"I just enjoy being able to help out," Fisher said. "Usually you get a lot more out of it than you put into it. It just puts things into perspective, and you feel fortunate about what you have. I just enjoy interacting mostly with kids."[5]

Mike also gained perspective on different parts of the world and different levels of need. The organization World Vision invited him to visit El Salvador.

Mike had sponsored children through World Vision by sending money, but seeing the poverty firsthand still came as a surprise. As he ducked in doorways and stood in shelters that barely cleared his head, he saw, touched, and felt how demanding life was. "Until you're here, it's hard to understand or explain."[6]

It's not out of the ordinary for food to run out completely or a family's well to run dry. A store wasn't just a few minutes away. Instead, villagers had to trek rough terrain to get bare basics like water and fruit. "It's a workout," Mike remarked. "It's pretty much up the side of a mountain."[7]

And Mike witnessed how a little charity can make big differences—helping a young girl set up a chicken farm, getting a tin roof over a family, starting a small

Photo provided by Jim and Karen Fisher

Mike with two young girls from El Salvador during his trip with World Vision.

market the size of a bathroom. "Right away you think about all the ways you waste money," he said, "but they could eat for a year. It puts things in perspective."[8]

Interestingly enough, Mike noticed that despite the tough circumstances, despair did not rule the day in El Salvador. The children smiled and played with him. "I think you can learn so much from the people here," he said. "They're very happy. They're very appreciative and thankful for even the little things that they have."[9]

"It was definitely eye-opening and life changing," Mike affirmed. "It made me want to help out, and I feel fortunate to be in a position that I could help."[10]

He didn't have to travel to another country to pitch in. Mike also helped at home. He served in a World Vision campaign to raise money for children like the ones he met in El Salvador. For each new child sponsored, he got to take a shot at a dunk tank. A bull's-eye would drop the host in a tank full of frigid water. So with nineteen new sponsorships, Mike got nineteen attempts to hit a target the size of a dinner plate.

"I've seen him shoot," the host said to the crowd from a vulnerable place over the water. "He might hit it once," he teased.

Mike laughed. "Cold?" he asked. "Alright." He used his hockey stick to toy with the ball for a second. *Wham!* Bull's-eye! The soaked host climbed up on the platform again. *Wham!* Two down, seventeen to go. The second time the host came out of the water and just looked at Mike. Seemed he didn't have much more to say.

Charity did feel good.

14

It's All Good

2009-2010

Before he could embark on his eleventh NHL season, Mike had to face some distractions. One of the Senators' top scorers wanted out of Ottawa. Fans felt betrayed. The press seethed. Mike managed more diplomacy.

"He's put the team in a predicament," Mike admitted. "We know that he can be such an asset. At the same time, we want people to be here that want to be here."[1]

Mike knew there was more to his job than producing on the ice. Whether facing tough losses, frustrating injuries, or locker-room disruptions, a professional represented the organization. A wise professional represented it well. In this case, Fisher resolved to take a page out of Roger Neilson's book—he had no bad words to say about a person.

The vast majority of reports fumed at the trade, citing the player's disloyalty and ego. But when the trade was finally granted, Mike commended his former teammate to the press. "He has done so much good here. He's a good guy ... he was a great teammate."[2]

After the trade, Mike became a regular alternate captain. He had worn the letter *A* for alternate captain eighteen times the previous season, but now he didn't have a jersey without it. "It's definitely a nice honor," Mike said, "but we have lots of guys who are leaders."[3]

Ottawa's head coach Cory Clouston was resolute. "He's a very good leader. He brings what we are looking for."[4]

"I'm not a rah-rah type of guy as far as leadership," said Mike. "I want to be a quiet, strong kind of leader. And off the ice, just try and lead by example, the way I live my life ... just be there for others, be a good friend and a good teammate."[5]

When the puck dropped on the year, Mike jumped into action.

Against the Islanders, Fish took the first shot of the OT — and scored the winner. He scored twice for a 3–2 win over the Leafs and recorded three assists in a game over Pittsburgh. By the end of November, he had earned four of which were game-winners, two in overtime. In December, he scored twice in a loss to the Kings. And he recorded points in five consecutive games. By the

Mike carrying the Olympic torch, 2009.

Andre Ringuette/Freestyle Photography; photo provided by Jim and Karen Fisher

Olympic break, he had scored thirty-one points in thirty-seven games and was seventeenth in the entire league on winning face-offs.

"I feel really good," Mike said at the time. "It's amazing what confidence will do. I feel now I'm playing offensively like I always knew I can. I definitely feel so much better with the puck ... I'm relaxed."[6]

Before the 2010 Vancouver games, Mike was asked to bring some Olympic spirit to Canada's Capital Region. So on a cold December evening in Ottawa, Fish took a turn carrying the Olympic flame in a coast-to-coast relay that would end up at the Vancouver opening ceremonies.

About the same time, Mike got another rare treat. The players' fathers were invited to join the team for a road trip. "They've all done so much for us when we were young," Mike said. "It's kind of nice for them to be able to see what they've helped us get to."[7]

The father/son trip had been planned since the summer, but Mike waited for the right time to pass on the invitation. When a teammate asked Mike's dad about it, Mr. Fisher didn't know anything about it. Later the Sens' captain mentioned it to Mr. Fisher again. "Mike turned to his teammate and said, 'That was his Christmas present from me!'"[8]

Even if the surprise didn't go as planned, it was still exciting for a father to see the details of his son's life on the road. "My dad has sacrificed a lot being a hockey dad, running me from rink to rink," said Mike, "so it's nice for him to enjoy this."[9]

Of course, the media reported the special road trip. But for a while, they had been buzzing about something entirely different. Mike always liked to talk to the press about hockey, but newspapers up north and magazines down south preferred to chat about his *musical tastes*. After some months of keeping a lid on it, country singer Carrie Underwood finally revealed that she and Mike were dating.

Poking fun at what she had heard about Mike before they met, she shared some lighthearted stories on a talk show. The glamorous singer punctuated her sentences with decidedly unglamorous razzes of her tongue. *He plays hockey?* [thumbs down and raspberry sound] *Did Mike have all his teeth?* [thumbs down and raspberry sound] *Did he live near her in Nashville?* [thumbs down and raspberry sound]

But the notes on Carrie's new CD put all teasing aside. "Thank you, #12," it read in part. "You are the most amazing addition to my life! I thank God for you every day."

In his own interview, Mike joked about the nice message, "I told her that when my CD came out, I'd return the favor," he laughed.[10]

Close to Christmas, Mike and Carrie got engaged. The crazy media circus was about to begin. (And Mike thought the hockey fans in Switzerland were nuts.)

Back at the rink, things cooled off a little after a smoking hot start, but Mike still drew the biggest stats

Larry Busacca/Getty Images for NARAS

Mike and Carrie during the 52nd Annual GRAMMY Awards — Salute to Icons Honoring Doug Morris — held at The Beverly Hilton Hotel on January 30, 2010, in Beverly Hills, California.

of his NHL career — most games played (79), most goals (25), most assists (28), most points (53). He led all Ottawa players in scoring and had six game-winners.

Mike explained that with other top scorers injured, along with regular shifts on the power play, he was really just stepping up for his team. "You know what ... guys were hurt," he said at the time. "I don't expect to lead the team (in goals). I'm going to do what I can do, but I'm not a top-scoring type of guy, especially on our team when guys are healthy."[11]

In April, the Sens got good news—they qualified for the playoffs. And they also received bad news—they would face the defending Cup champions, the Pittsburgh Penguins, in the first round.

The Senators went on the road and took the lead to stun everyone with a game one 5–4 win. After they lost the second road game, they went back to Ottawa—and lost two more. Suddenly, the Sens were down in the series 3 to 1.

On the road again for game five, they had to score, scrape, and scrap to stay alive. Mike scored first on the power play, and after one period, the Sens were up by a goal. After two periods, the teams were tied at two goals apiece. By the end of regulation time, each team had three. Both teams battled and banged through overtime ... still tied. They fought through a second OT ... still tied. Then seven minutes into the third OT, just before midnight, the Sens sent it back home with the strong, critical win.

In game six, they held a lead most of the game but couldn't keep it. After the dramatic victory in game five, the tables turned. They had pushed the favored Penguins to an unexpected six games but lost in a tough OT period 3–4.

Like hunting for bear in Alaska or playing soccer with kids in El Salvador, Mike's 2010 summer adventure was once-in-a-lifetime. He got married.

With Warren as his best man, Mike and Carrie said their vows under a tent in Georgia surrounded by family and friends. "I was thanking God for her, for that moment," said Mike. "It's something I'll never forget."[12]

For a solid month, both Canada and the US dwelled on details of rings and dresses and a barking dog in a pink tux. But when asked by the press about details, Mike seemed puzzled. "What wedding?"[13] he asked straight-faced before breaking into a smile.

Mike admitted that he was his wife's biggest fan. And she was his. "Mike is such a strong person," Carrie said. "And he talks about his faith openly. He doesn't go around making people feel bad, but when he's asked, he's honest. That's how I want to be."[14]

Before they met, Mike had always been decidedly quiet about personal details. He was happy to be accessible to fans, but he preferred private things to stay private. Now he was married to a public figure and different lines had to be drawn. He could fight the intrusive media scrutiny in a losing battle, or he could adjust. "I'm learning to deal with it," he said. "It's a part of life now, I guess. You can use it for good or bad too."[15]

Be glad for all God is planning for you ... Romans 12:12.

When he entered the league, Mike was young and shy, but he stepped up to be a well-spoken, approachable leader. During his early years as a pro, he was private but accepted the attention that came with interested fans.

Now he stepped into a wider, brighter spotlight with his celebrity wife. "You just kind of learn to live with it," he said. "It's all good. It's all worth it."[16]

After the honeymoon, Mike went directly to his hockey school. The camp sessions continued to thrive as they welcomed new kids, campers who had been there before, players from Canada, and youth from overseas.

Mike and Carrie Fisher teamed up for charity too. Along with some Ottawa teammates, the couple raised money for the local children's hospital. Altogether, tens of thousands of dollars were raised. Teamwork was a beautiful thing.

15

Fearless Enough to Follow

2010–2011

As always, when training camp rolled around, Mike was excited and ready to lace up his skates. "I always want to be better at everything," he said. "Every year at the end of the year, I want to do a few things better—better offensively, better in certain areas, be a more complete player. I'm usually my worst critic, but last year was my best season offensively. But after the season I had before, I just came in more relaxed, just wanted to play, not overthink the game and how the team did, so I want to do the same this year. I'm just looking forward to it. I want to be the best I can be."[1]

The Senators started training at Canadian Forces Base Petawawa (commonly referred to as CFG Petawawa), where the team trained like part of the military. They all had a part to play, had to be ready to play it, had to come together as a team.

Early in the season, Mike crashed into the boards headfirst and tweaked his neck and clavicle. It didn't stop him, but he had to play it safe. "A lot of time you get your adrenaline and your legs from being physical and being able to forecheck, and right now I'm not able to do that," he said. "It's kind of frustrating, because for me to be effective, my game is getting in the traffic areas. It's not a perimeter game. It's kind of what I feel I have to be right now."[2]

So he focused on getting shots on net—four shots in a loss to Buffalo and ... eight shots in a win over the Hurricanes. Sometimes the puck would go between the pipes, sometimes it wouldn't, but he knew he had to keep looking for chances.

The old rival Maple Leafs seemed to bring out his best. At the beginning of November, Fish took a pass through the defense and motored to the goal. A burst of speed gave him a breakaway, leaving a desperate defenseman only one choice—hook Fisher to keep him from getting off the shot. The refs whistled for a penalty shot. Starting at center, Mike carried the puck at the netminder and went top shelf with a quick flick of the wrist.

In their next matchup at the end of November, Mike started a play on one knee behind his own goal. He came out on defense, read the play, and charged up ice. Making a kick pass, Fish battled against a Leaf who tried to take him down. He got the pass, drew the goalie out, and moved the puck left to backhand it into the net.

Shifts like that helped Mike's line get all three points for the win that night.

Despite the team's efforts, Ottawa was punished for every turnover and paid for every mistake. "We've definitely struggled with a lot of inconsistencies and haven't played near the hockey we know we're capable of," Mike explained. "Some nights it's there. Other nights, it's 'Where'd we go?' "[3] Like running on ice, the tireless work got them nowhere.

"We haven't quit by any means," said Mike. "We're in a position we don't like, but it's a good opportunity to show our character and battle back."[4]

When his team didn't live up to the expectations of spectators—and of *themselves*—Fish tried to play more physically, despite his soreness. By the end of October, he had twenty-one hits to tie with teammate Chris Neil (the undisputed champion of penalty minutes year after year—and the prankster responsible for the boy-band stickers on Fisher's helmet). His clavicle took longer to heal, but he and his teammates were trying to get some wins, some confidence, and some momentum.

The only momentum they managed was in the loss column, though. During January, Ottawa suffered its longest losing streak since the early '90s. Mike focused on the little things—each shift, each period, each positive step. And he also focused on the big picture—the God who never changes was still in control.

In January, Mike was asked if he had any New Year's resolutions. He took a second, "Forget 2010?" he half-joked.

Then he quickly corrected himself, "On the ice, I mean," he laughed.

The Senators' team effort had more success off the ice. Mike and Carrie joined the other couples from the team along with the Senators Foundation to help the organization raise one million dollars for charity. The season proved to be a tough year inside the arena but definitely worth celebrating away from it.

On Thursday, February 10, the Senators were in the middle of a demanding four-game road trip. One hour before the morning skate in Calgary, Ottawa's general manager delivered some startling news. The Nashville Predators had called to make a deal. They had come up with the resources, and they wanted Fisher. Mike had just been traded.

Known by one headline as "the trade that shook Ottawa,"[5] the news rattled the region. Changes were no surprise to the Senators, especially after the difficult year they'd had. But no one predicted a move for the alternate captain, who was lauded as a fan-favorite and valued teammate. Just a couple of weeks before, the general manager himself predicted that number twelve was in Ottawa to stay.

But with two months left in the regular season, instead of going to practice, Mike was getting on a plane.

"Well," he said with a smile that barely disguised the emotions just under the surface, "it's very hard for sure.

It's a bit of a shock. I'm still trying to process everything. I don't know if it's really set in yet. I wish I could have done more here. I wanted to be a part of everything here, but it wasn't meant to be.[6]

"I've got so many things to be grateful for playing in Ottawa," Mike continued. "It's been a great ride. Fans have been great. The organization has been first class. I've played with so many great players and people. The hardest part is the good-byes to people, that's what it's all about. Yeah, it's tough."[7]

Taking a deep breath during the next question, Mike focused on his future in Nashville (where his wife already worked in the music industry). "I'm excited about that. If there's a place I was to go, it would be there. I'm excited about being part of that team. They're a very good team. It will be kind of like going home for me. It's a great place for me and my family and everything."[8]

Although reeling from the sudden developments and overwhelmed with mixed emotions, Mike's practice of professionalism took over. To the community of Ottawa and broader fan base of the Senators, he looked in the camera and said, "Thanks for eleven great years. I wish I could have done more. For me it was so many great memories that I'll never forget. Thank you so much."[9]

The move set off a mad swirl of activity. All of a sudden there was family to notify, good-byes to rush through, people to meet, interviews to do, work visas to apply for, bags to pack ... But during the plane ride and the drive home before he went to Tennessee, Mike was able to absorb some of the implications.

By moving from north to south of the Canadian border, he also transferred from the eastern to the western conference in the NHL. Ottawa played some of the teams in the west only once a year, so a lot of the names and faces were unfamiliar. But a couple of Mike's new Nashville teammates, along with the coach, were with Team Canada at the 2009 World Championships in Switzerland. And he knew some others from the practice ice when he spent some summer months in Nashville with Carrie. "Obviously, having a house here makes the transition a lot easier than coming being in a hotel not knowing anyone," he said.[10]

Of course the hockey promised to be fun. "I knew what style they play, so I knew coming in I'd be a good fit. They're a good hard-working team and I thought I could add to that."[11]

"I just want to play hard and help them the best I can," said Nashville's new number twelve.[12]

And while the Senators' chances of making the playoffs had disappeared, the Predators still had a promise of a postseason. "There's a lot to play for here," Mike said. "It's a different feeling. All these games are so important with the team in the playoff race."[13]

Mike took out a full-page ad in the Ottawa paper to thank the community, to commemorate their shared history of sport and charity, and to provide some closure that was impossible in a mid-season trade.

And then he turned and faced the rest of the season.

Mike Fisher (#12) in his first game as a member of the Nashville Predators on February 12, 2011.

Two days after the trade, Mike was on the ice in Nashville. Captain Shea Weber, one of his new teammates who had played with him in Switzerland, expressed the team's excitement: "Everyone knows what [Mike] can do on the ice. He can do everything. He kills penalties, he can play on the power play. He's a big body up front. He has been to the Stanley Cup Finals, so that's a lot of experience. He's played well in the playoffs, too. That's invaluable and something you can't find in a lot of places."[14]

On February 12 Nashville fans got to express their appreciation of the trade as well. In the Predators' game against Colorado, signs dotted the glass in warm-ups: "Hey, Mike, Welcome to Smashville!"

The fans celebrated right through Fisher's first game in a blue jersey. In the 5–3 win, Mike got an assist, won 75 percent of his face-offs, and screened the goaltender for a first period goal. "I got to play with ... two skilled guys who make it kind of easy for a new guy coming in," he said, affirming the team. "Obviously getting the win made it feel great—a lot of relief after that."[15]

Five days later, the Predators faced off against the Vancouver Canucks, the team with the most points in the NHL. Midway through the first period, Mike took a puck to the cheek and left the ice. "It took awhile to get stitched up, but after that it was just stopping the bleeding," he said. "I felt fine."[16]

He felt fine enough to score a beauty. With only forty-nine seconds left in the second period, Mike got a stick on a Predator slap shot that surprised the netminder. "It was a pretty good tip by him, reaching out and deflecting it with the tip of his stick back towards the net," admitted Vancouver's goalie, Roberto Luongo. "I didn't see if it was a hand pass or not, but it was a pretty good play by Fisher."[17] A good play that iced the win for Nashville.

Ultimately the challenges—both good and bad, hard and exciting—didn't upset Mike's faith in the God of all things. To a reporter the defender of faith simply acknowledged, "You never do know what the good Lord has in store."[18]

The wild rollercoaster of the NHL rolls on. And it's not for the wimpy.

At the end of the 2012 season, the league will be talking money again. Players and owners will have to agree on terms, like they tried to do during the lockout.

In the summer of 2013, Mike's contract will be up for negotiation. At thirty-three, he and his team will decide what to do with his blessings and his assets.

Like previous years, the unknowns and distractions make life a lot like balancing on Jell-O in a blizzard at midnight. A new wife, a new city, and new teammates may have come into Mike's life, but through the storm God remains the anchor in his life. Mike has proven that he's willing to go where God takes him, courageous enough to follow, and committed to seeing what's ahead.

Fisher's God-given gifts of playing hockey have led him on this adventure. And it's far from over. *Be glad for all God is planning for you. Be patient in trouble, and always be prayerful.*

Romans 12:12.

World Vision

Who we are

World Vision is a Christian humanitarian organization dedicated to working with children, families, and their communities worldwide to reach their full potential by tackling the causes of poverty and injustice.

Who we serve

We serve close to 100 million people in nearly 100 countries around the world. World Vision serves all people, regardless of religion, race, ethnicity, or gender.

Why we serve

Motivated by our faith in Jesus Christ, we serve alongside the poor and oppressed as a demonstration of God's unconditional love for all people.

Reflecting Christ in each community

Wherever we work, our prayer is that our efforts will be used by God to heal and strengthen people's relationships with Him and with one another. We do this by demonstrating God's unconditional love for all people through our service to the poor—which includes providing for daily needs, working to build peace and promote justice, and partnering with churches and individuals to encourage spiritual transformation.

Reaching around the globe

World Vision is a global organization with offices in approximately 100 countries. These interdependent national offices are bound together by a Covenant of Partnership, a biblically based agreement that enables us to work together in a unified and complementary way as we walk alongside those we serve.

Employing the best in every region

We are blessed with staff who are experts in a broad range of technical specialties, ranging from hydrology to microenterprise development to public health. And we are inspired by the ways in which they use their God-given abilities in conjunction with existing community resources. Of the more than 40,000 staff employed by World Vision, 97 percent work in their home countries or regions. Familiar with the culture and language, they bring to World Vision a deeply personal understanding of how best to assist local children and families.

Meeting diverse needs

The millions of people we serve include earthquake and hurricane survivors, abandoned and exploited children, survivors of famine and civil war, refugees, and children and families in communities devastated by AIDS in Africa, Asia, and Latin America. Our extensive global infrastructure enables us to respond where the need is greatest, anywhere in the world.

Trusted worldwide

The excellence of World Vision's work has earned the trust of more than 3 million donors, supporters, and volunteers; more than half a million child sponsors; thousands of churches; hundreds of corporations; and government agencies in the United States and around the world. We are thankful to God that through these collaborative efforts, we are able to be a part of breaking the cycle of poverty for those in need in our world.

Endnotes

Chapter 1: Some Kind of Pain

1. "Mike Fisher Story," YouTube video, 4:12, posted by "unikrahn," August 2, 2007, http://www.youtube.com /watch?v=Imzk-hI44aY.

2. Ibid.

3. Ibid.

Chapter 2: Where It All Started

1. Lois Thomson, "Fisher & Faith, Grit & Grace," Living Light News, accessed March 15, 2011, http://www.livinglightnews .org/vfisher.htm.

2. Tom McGough, "Mike Fisher Power Play Interview," YouTube video, 4:01, from Sports Week, posted by "chadillachembree," June 1, 2010, http://www.youtube.com /watch?v=nS0N9dwmOcg.

3. Mike Fisher, in discussion with the author, January 6, 2011.

4. Ibid.

5. Ibid.

6. Ibid.

7. "Hunting with Mike Fisher," YouTube video, 4:49, from SENS TV, posted by "volchassa," September 18, 2009, http://www.youtube.com/watch?v=44Nr2iYjdJY&feature =related.

8. Mike Fisher, in discussion with the author, January 6, 2011.

9. Mike Fisher, "Testimony," *The Official Mike Fisher Website,* accessed March 15, 2011, http://www.mikefisher.ca/testimony.

10. Thomson, "Fisher & Faith, Grit & Grace," http:// www.livinglightnews.org/vfisher.htm.

Chapter 3: Make It or Break It

1. "Peterborough Petes," Wikipedia, last modified on February 10, 2011, http://en.wikipedia.org/wiki/Peterborough_Petes.
2. Jennifer Green, "Mike Fisher on Faith," Ottawa Citizen. com, March 5, 2009, http://www.ottawacitizen.com/Mike +Fisher+faith+Senators+star+keeps+grounded/1474147 /story.html.
3. Ibid.
4. "Mike Fisher Story," http://www.youtube.com /watch?v=Imzk-hI44aY.
5. Rob Brodie, "Big Hits, Bigger Heart," OttawaSenators.com, July 7, 2007, http://senators.nhl.com/club/news .htm?id=480230.
6. Mike Fisher, in discussion with the author, January 6, 2011.
7. "Catching Up with Fish," The Official Mike Fisher Website, June 26, 2010, http://www.mikefisher.ca/news/155/.
8. "Mike Fisher's Fan Shootout Answers," e.com, February 13, 2007, http://www.thehockeynews.com/articles/9643-Mike -Fishers-Fan-Shootout-answers.html.
9. "More Mike!," The Official Mike Fisher Website, October 27, 2009, http://www.mikefisher.ca/news/54/.

Chapter 4: Big Time with the Big Boys

1. "Mike Fisher: Draft Day Memories," YouTube video, 1:27, posted by "friskie1986," June 24, 2008, http://www.youtube .com/watch?v=d7NXoarx8Ls.
2. "Mike Fisher Player Bio," *TheHockeyNews.com*, http:// forecaster.thehockeynews.com/hockeynews/hockey/player .cgi?1317.
3. "Mike Fisher Talks to Reporters about his New Wife," CTV Ottawa, CTV Globe Media, July 28, 2010, http://ottawa.ctv. ca/servlet/an/local/CTVNews/20100728/OTT_Fisher_100 728/20100728/?hub=OttawaHome.

4. Green, "Mike Fisher on Faith," http://www.ottawacitizen.com
/Mike+Fisher+faith+Senators+star+keeps+grounded
/1474147/story.html.http://www.ottawacitizen.com/Mike+
Fisher+faith+Senators+star+keeps+grounded/1474147
/story.html.

5. Barre Campbell, "Fisher proves he's NHL worthy to Sens,"
Ottawa Sun, November 5, 1999, http://www.sensplayers.com
/mikefisher/news_991105.html.

6. Don Brennan, "Q&A with Mike Fisher," *Ottawa Sun,*
March 23, 2003. http://www.sensplayers.com/mikefisher
/news_030323.html.

7. Thomson, "Fisher & Faith, Grit & Grace," http://
www.livinglightnews.org/vfisher.htm.

8. SENSTV online, *The Sens Show,* Episode 3, October 31,
1999.

9. Campbell, "Fisher Proves He's NHL Worthy to Sens,"
http://www.sensplayers.com/mikefisher/news_991105.html.

10. Thomson, "Fisher & Faith, Grit & Grace," http://
www.livinglightnews.org/vfisher.htm.

11. "Fishing for Success," *NHLPA.com*, National Hockey League
Players' Association, http://nhlpa.com/News/Headlines/
E56E2D30-C38A-4670-AD18-E7D37CE4A15A/Fishing
-for-Success.

12. Ibid.

13. Thomson, "Fisher & Faith, Grit & Grace," http://
www.livinglightnews.org/vfisher.htm.

Chapter 5: More Than Me, Me, Me

1. "Fishing for Success," http://nhlpa.com/News/Headlines
/E56E2D30-C38A-4670-AD18-E7D37CE4A15A/Fishing
-for-Success.

2. "More Mike!," http://www.mikefisher.ca/news/54/.

3. "Mike Fisher's Fan Shootout Answers," *The Hockey News,*
The Hockey News Corporation, February 13, 2007,

http://www.thehockeynews.com/articles/9643-Mike-Fish-ers-Fan-Shootout-answers.html.

4. "Mike Fisher," *Tothenextlevel.org*, TTNL Sports Network, http://www.tothenextlevel.org/docs/testimonies/testimonies_hockey/fisher_mike/fisher_mike_%20default.asp.

5. "Mike Fisher and Chris Neil Are Harassed by Mark Hatfield," YouTube video, 4:50, from *Big Bad Sports Show*, posted by Mark Hatfield66, January 21, 2010, http://www.youtube.com/watch?v=qmY6HiL33lg.

6. Mike Fisher, in discussion with the author, January 6, 2011.

7. Green, "Mike Fisher on Faith," http://www.ottawacitizen.com/Mike+Fisher+faith+Senators+star+keeps+grounded/1474147/story.html.

8. Ibid.

9. Mike Fisher, in discussion with the author, January 6, 2011.

10. Ibid.

11. "Catching Up with Fish," http://www.mikefisher.ca/.

12. Thomson, "Fisher & Faith, Grit & Grace," http://www.livinglightnews.org/vfisher.htm.

Chapter 6: Number 12 and Captain Video

1. Green, "Mike Fisher on Faith," http://www.ottawacitizen.com/Mike+Fisher+faith+Senators+star+keeps+grounded/1474147/story.html.

2. "Mike Fisher Story," http://www.youtube.com/watch?v=Imzk-hI44aY.

3. "Peterborough Petes," *Wikipedia,* http://en.wikipedia.org/wiki/Peterborough_Petes. http.

4. Bill Kellet, "Stuff of Legends: Roger Neilson," *TheHockeyGuys.com*, May 13, 2010, http://thehockeyguys.net/?p=1183.

5. Ibid.

6. "Fishing for Success," http://nhlpa.com/News/Headlines/
   E56E2D30-C38A-4670-AD18-E7D37CE4A15A/Fishing-for-
   Success.

Chapter 7: Fight the Good Fight, Keep the Faith

1. "Interview—Mike Fisher," http://ilikemike12.blogspot.com,
   February 8, 2008, http://ilikemike12.blogspot.com/2008/02
   /interview-mike-fisher.html.
2. Fisher, Mike, "Testimony," http://www.mikefisher.ca
   /testimony/.
3. Green, "Mike Fisher on Faith," http://www.ottawacitizen.com
   /Mike+Fisher+faith+Senators+star+keeps+grounded
   /1474147/story.html.
4. Mike Fisher, in discussion with the author, January 6, 2011.
5. McGough, "Mike Fisher Power Play Interview," http://
   www.youtube.com/watch?v=nS0N9dwmOcg.

Chapter 8: The Arm Is Strong but It Ain't Straight

1. Mike Fisher, in discussion with the author, January 6, 2011.
2. "Interview—Mike Fisher," http://ilikemike12.blogspot.com.
3. Mike Fisher, in discussion with the author, January 6, 2011.
4. http://www.youtube.com/watch?v=KY0V6HLkTwc
   Originally aired on Rogers Sportsnet.
5. "Fisher King: Mike Fisher proves worthy guardian of Sens'
   hockey Grail hopes," Canadian Press, April 19, 2004, http://
   www.sensplayers.com/mikefisher.
6. Mike Fisher, in discussion with the author, January 6, 2011.
7. Ibid.

Chapter 9: Raise Your Sticks and Smack the Glass

1. Ibid.
2. Ibid.
3. Ibid.

4. Ibid.
5. Ibid.
6. Ibid.

Chapter 10: 12:12

1. "Catching Up with Fish." http://www.mikefisher.ca/.
2. Don Brennan, "Hanging With the Big Fish," *Canoe Network, Slam Sports,* September 16, 2006, http://slam.canoe.ca/Slam /Columnists/Brennan/2006/09/16/1848606-sun.html.
3. Ibid.
4. Tony Care, "Emerging From Obscurity — Ottawa centre Mike Fisher thrives in faster NHL," CBC Sports, June 1, 2007, http://ilikemike12.blogspot.com/2007/06/emerging -from-obscurity-ottawa-centre.html.
5. "Mike Fisher Profile," *Senators.nhl.com*, May 5, 2005, http:// video.senators.nhl.com/videocenter/console?id=17644.
6. "Mike Fisher Story" http://www.youtube.com/watch?v =Imzk-hI44aY.
7. Ibid.
8. Bruce Garrioch, "Fisher Catches Big Break," *Canoe Network, Slam Sports*, March 18, 2006, http://slam.canoe.ca/Slam /Hockey/NHL/Ottawa/2006/03/18/1494250-sun.html.
9. Ibid.
10. "Sens Skills Competition Part 5 of 8," YouTube video, 9:12, from Sensnetwork.com, posted by "sensnetwork.com," February 18, 2008, http://www.youtube.com/watch?v =qtwBBDXi0kg.
11. Ibid.
12. http://ilikemike12.blogspot.com/2006/05/end-of-season .html.
13. Mike Fisher, in discussion with the author, January 6, 2011.

Endnotes

Chapter 11: The Senators and Lord Stanley

1. "Mike Fisher on TSN's OTR," YouTube video, 0:32, from TSN.ca, posted by "jasonboucher," May 27, 2007, http://www.youtube.com/watch?v=Gg_JyebdyYE.

2. Mike Fisher, in discussion with the author, January 6, 2011.

3. Ken Warren, "Senators Give Elgin the Star Treatment," *The Ottawa Sun and Ottawa Citizen,* April 5, 2007, Page: A1 / FRONT, Edition: Final.

4. "Mike Fisher Profile," Senators.nhl.com, May 5, 2005, http://video.senators.nhl.com/videocenter/console?id=17644.

5. Ibid.

6. Warren, "Senators Give Elgin the Star Treatment," *The Ottawa Sun and Ottawa Citizen,* April 5, 2007,Page: A1 / FRONT, Edition: Final.

7. Mike Fisher, in discussion with the author, January 6, 2011.

8. "Three-Year-Old Succumbed to Cancer Two Hours After His Favorite Team Won," *The Ottawa Citizen*, May 20, 2007, http://www.canada.com/ottawacitizen/story.html?id=9f4cdd28-4c01-4b80-87c1-042c6d614fe4&k=20956.

9. "Anaheim Ducks–Ottawa Senators Scrum," YouTube video, 2:03, from hockeyfights.com, posted by "hockeyfightsdotcom," June 2, 2007, http://www.youtube.com/watch?v=tTAZqCdHmD0.

10. Roy MacGregor, "MacGregor: 'I Like to Think I Give Everything I Have,' Fisher Says," from Globe and Mail, July 8, 2007, http://ilikemike12.blogspot.com/2007/07/macgregor-i-like-to-think-i-give.html.

11. Emily Wierenga, "Faithful Fisher," *Christianity.ca*, May 2008, http://www.christianity.ca/netcommunity/page.aspx?pid=6168.

12. MacGregor, "MacGregor: 'I like to Think,'" http://ilikemike12.blogspot.com/2007/07/macgregor-i-like-to-think-i-give.html.

13. Mike Fisher, in discussion with the author, January 6, 2011.

Chapter 12: Scores and Scraps

1. "Mike Fisher Profile," http://video.senators.nhl.com /videocenter/console?id=17644.
2. Fisher, "Testimony,"http://www.mikefisher.ca/.
3. "The Code, God—Stu Grimson," YouTube video, 3:20, posted by "Humpzilla21," January 1, 2009, http:// www.youtube.com/watch?v=fesy4muDrVg.
4. Mike Fisher, in discussion with the author, January 6, 2011.
5. "Senators All Access Dec 29th 2007," Senators.nhl.com, 6:29, January 3, 2008, http://video.senators.nhl.com /videocenter/console?id=10097.
6. Green, "Mike Fisher on Faith," http://www.ottawacitizen.com /Mike+Fisher+faith+Senators+star+keeps+grounded /1474147/story.html.
7. "Interview—Mike Fisher." http://ilikemike12.blogspot.com /2008/02/interview-mike-fisher.html
8. "Mike Fisher's Hockey Camp," Senators.nhl.com, 2:19. Posted August 27, 2008, http://video.senators.nhl.com /videocenter/console?id=20393.
9. Ibid.

Chapter 13: I'll Play Anywhere

1. Allen Panzeri, "Fisher's line shows promise for Sens," *Canwest News Service*, October 12, 2008, http://ilikemike12 .blogspot.com/2008_10_01_archive.html.
2. Bruce Garrioch, "Go Fish! He's back in lineup," *Ottawa Sun*, October 11, 2008, http://www.hs.facebook.com /note.php?note_id=65936144992.
3. Andrew Podnieks, "Pure Gold: Russia Repeats," International Ice Hockey Federation, May 10, 2009, http:// www.iihf.com/channels/iihf-world-championship-oc09 /home/news/news-singleview-world-championship-2009 /article/pure-gold-russia-repeats.html.
4. Ibid.

5. Rob Brodie, "Getting to know ... Mike Fisher: There's much more to Sens centre than his hard-working play," *OttawaSenators.com*, September 12, 2009, http://senators.nhl.com/club/news.htm?id=509203.

6. "Childview Winter 2010/11: Mike Fisher in El Salvador," YouTube video, 2:43, from World Vision Canada, posted by "worldvisioncanada," October 13, 2010, http://www.youtube.com/watch?v=ctwtZD_2AnI.

7. "Fisher Sees Poverty Firsthand," *The Official Mike Fisher Website,* October 17, 2009. http://www.mikefisher.ca/news/44.

8. Ibid.

9. Ibid.

10. Ibid.

Chapter 14: It's All Good

1. M. P. Kelly, "Exclusive Interview with Mike Fisher: It will be a circus," *TheHockeyWriters.com*, September 10, 2009, http://thehockeywriters.com/exclusive-interview-with-mike-fisher-it-will-be-a-circus.

2. Peter Raaymakers, "Fisher 'surprised' and 'upset' by Heatley's trade demand," *Ottawa Sun*, June 12, 2009, http://www.silversevensens.com/2009/6/12/907347/fisher-surprised-and-upset-by.

3. Mike Fisher, in discussion with the author, January 6, 2011.

4. "Fisher named alternate captain," *The Official Mike Fisher Website,* October 2, 2009, http://www.mikefisher.ca/news/32/.

5. McGough, "YouTube, Power Play Interview," http://www.youtube.com/watch?v=nS0N9dwmOcg.

6. Don Brennan, "Fisher talks about Underwood," *Sun Media*, November 23, 2009, http://ilikemike12.blogspot.com/2009/11/fisher-talks-about-underwood.html.

7. Don Brennan, "A little Son-shine for Sens' dads," *OttawaSun.com*, January 17, 2010, http://www.ottawasun.com/sports/columnists/don_brennan/2010/01/16/12495496.html.

8. Ibid.

9. "Father and Son hit the road," *The Official Mike Fisher Website,* January 15, 2010, http://www.mikefisher.ca/news/98.

10. Brennan, "Fisher talks about Underwood," http://ilikemike12.blogspot.com/2009/11/fisher-talks-about-underwood.html.

11. Wayne Scanlan, "Life in the Fishbowl," *The Ottawa Citizen*, September 28, 2010, http://ilikemike12.blogspot.com/.

12. Tony Lofaro, "Carrie Underwood and Mike Fisher nuptials make cover of *People* magazine," The Vancouver Sun, July 14, 2010, http://www.vancouversun.com/entertainment/Carrie+Underwood+Mike+Fisher+nuptials+make+cover+People+magazine/3276581/story.html.

13. "Mike Fisher CTV Ottawa Interview talks about his wife Carrie Underwood (AKA Fisher)," YouTube video, 8:07, posted by "roxygirly12," August 1, 2010, http://www.youtube.com/watch?v=oeCuTSdk8UI&playnext=1&list=PLABF1492408949B53.

14. Bruce Ward, "For Carrie Underwood, hubby hockey star Mike Fisher 'makes me a better person,'" *Postmedia News,* October 14, 2010, http://ilikemike12.blogspot.com/2010/11/for-carrie-underwood-hubby-hockey-star.html.

15. "Mike Fisher CTV Ottawa Interview talks about his wife Carrie Underwood (AKA Fisher)," http://www.youtube.com/watch?v=oeCuTSdk8UI&playnext=1&list=PLABF1492408949B53.

16. Ibid.

Chapter 15: Fearless Enough to Follow

1. Ibid.

2. Allen Panzeri, "Sens' Fisher playing through injury," *The Ottawa Citizen*, November 18, 2010, http://www2.canada.com /topics/sports/story.html?id=3851297.

3. "Interview with Gord Wilson," *Ottawasenators.com,* http:// video.senators.nhl.com/videocenter/console?id=87525.

4. Allen Panzeri, "Struggling Sens saying all the right things ..." *The Gazette,* January 3, 2011, http://www.ottawacitizen.com /sports/Sens+they+haven+quit+coach/4054032/story.html.

5. Bryan Mullen, "Mike Fisher Already Feeling Right at Home," *The Tennessean*, February 13, 2011.

6. "Mike Fisher reacts to trade," *The Official Mike Fisher Website,* from NHL Network Online, February 10, 2011, http:// www.mikefisher.ca/news/242.

7. Ibid.

8. Ibid.

9. Ibid.

10. "Interview with Terry Crisp," *http://predators.nhl.com,* February 15, 2011, http://www.mikefisher.ca/news/246.

11. Ibid.

12. Bryan Mullen, "Mike Fisher Already Feeling Right at Home," *The Tennessean*, February 13, 2011.

13. "Fisher to make Nashville debut," *The Official Mike Fisher Website,* February 12, 2011, http://www.mikefisher.ca/news /244.

14. Bryan Mullen, "Mike Fisher Already Feeling Right at Home," *The Tennessean,* February 13, 2011.

15. "Interview with Terry Crisp," http://predators.nhl.com. http://www.mikefisher.ca/news/246.

16. "Predators 3, Canucks 1," Associated Press, *predators.nhl.com,* http://predators.nhl.com/club/recap.htm?id=2010020866.

17. Ibid.

18. Don Brennan, "Fisher: I'm So Grateful to Ottawa," *Ottawa Sun*, February 10, 2011, http://www.ottawasun.com/sports /hockey/2011/02/10/17232836.html.

We want to hear from you. Please send your comments about this book to us in care of zreview@zondervan.com. Thank you.